Collins

INTERNATIONAL
PRIMARY
MATHS

Student's Book 6

William Collins' dream of knowledge for all began with the publication of his first book in 1819. A self-educated mill worker, he not only enriched millions of lives, but also founded a flourishing publishing house. Today, staying true to this spirit, Collins books are packed with inspiration, innovation and practical expertise. They place you at the centre of a world of possibility and give you exactly what you need to explore it.

Collins. Freedom to teach.

An imprint of HarperCollins*Publishers*
The News Building
1 London Bridge Street
London
SE1 9GF

Browse the complete Collins catalogue at www.collins.co.uk

British Library Cataloguing in Publication Data
A catalogue record for this publication is available from the British Library.

Publishing manager Fiona McGlade
Series editor Peter Clarke
Managing editor Caroline Green
Editor Kate Ellis
Project managed by Emily Hooton
Developed by Joan Miller, Tracy Thomas and Karen Williams
Edited by Tanya Solomons
Proofread by Emily Hooton and Tracy Thomas
Cover design by Amparo Barrera
Cover artwork by Katseyephoto/Dreamstime.com
Internal design by Ken Vail Graphic Design Ltd
Typesetting by Ken Vail Graphic Design Ltd
Illustrations by Ken Vail Graphic Design Ltd, Advocate Art and Beehive Illustration
Production by Lauren Crisp

Printed and bound by Grafica Veneta S. P. A.

Contents

Number

Geometry

Measure

Handling data

Lesson 1: **Counting on and back**

Number

- Count forwards and backwards in multiples of powers of 10 to 100 000

Key words
- thousands
- ten thousands
- hundred thousands
- place value
- power of ten
- boundary

Discover

$22 294

Learn

You can use knowledge of place value to count on in multiples of 10, 100 or 1000. Focus on how the digits change, particularly when you cross a tens boundary.

The person buying the car has paid a deposit of $10 294. She wants to pay the outstanding amount in $100 bills. Imagine how much time it would take to count from 0 to add the remaining $12 000!

Describe what happens when you count on from 67 342 in thousands.

6	7	3	4	2
6	8	3	4	2
6	9	3	4	2
7	0	3	4	2
7	1	3	4	2

When the count crosses the ten thousands boundary, the ten thousands digit increases by 1 and the thousands digit resets to 0.

1

Number

Lesson 2: **Place value**

- Know what each digit represents in whole numbers up to a million

Key words
- thousands
- ten thousands
- hundred thousands
- place value

Discover

The values of the digits 4 and 3 in the number 43 570 are 40 000 and 3000.

4	3	5	7	0

4	0	0	0	0	= 40 thousands

3	0	0	0	= 3 thousands

Learn

You can think of a number as being made up of several parts.

How can you split up 689 321?

689 321 can be thought of as 689 thousands and 321 ones.

6689 321 can also be thought of as 6 hundred thousands, 89 ten thousands, 3 hundreds and 21.

You can also think of 689 321 as 68 ten thousands, 9 thousands and 321 ones.

Lesson 3: **Multiplying and dividing by 10, 100 or 1000**

- Multiply and divide any whole number from 1 to 10 000 by 10, 100 or 1000 and explain the effect

Discover

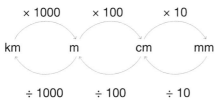

```
    × 1000     × 100      × 10
  km       m        cm       mm
    ÷ 1000     ÷ 100      ÷ 10
```

Learn

Multiply by 10:   Move the digits one place value to the left.

Multiply by 100:   Move the digits 2 place values to the left.

Multiply by 1000:   Move the digits 3 place values to the left.

M	HTh	TTh	Th	H	T	U	
			7	4	3	6	
		7	4	3	6	0	× 10
	7	4	3	6	0	0	× 100
7	4	3	6	0	0	0	× 1000

Divide by 10:   Move the digits one place value to the right.

Divide by 100:   Move the digits 2 place values to the right.

Divide by 1000:   Move the digits 3 place values to the right.

HTh	TTh	Th	H	T	U	
		3	0	0	0	
			3	0	0	÷ 10
				3	0	÷ 100
					3	÷ 1000

Example

Work out 7436 × 1000 and 3000 ÷ 1000.

M	HTh	TTh	Th	H	T	U		HTh	TTh	Th	H	T	U
			7	4	3	6				3	0	0	0
		7	4	3	6	0					3	0	0
	7	4	3	6	0	0						3	0
7	4	3	6	0	0	0							3

Lesson 4: **Factors and multiples**

Number

* Find factors of 2-digit numbers
* Find some common multiples of pairs of numbers

Discover

Factors and multiples have an inverse relationship –
if A is a **multiple** of B, then B is a **factor** of A.

$1 \times 6 = 6$	$1 \times 7 = 7$	$1 \times 8 = 8$	$1 \times 9 = 9$	$1 \times 10 = 10$
$2 \times 6 = 12$	$2 \times 7 = 14$	$2 \times 8 = 16$	$2 \times 9 = 18$	$2 \times 10 = 20$
$3 \times 6 = 18$	$3 \times 7 = 21$	$3 \times 8 = 24$	$3 \times 9 = 27$	$3 \times 10 = 30$
$4 \times 6 = 24$	$4 \times 7 = 28$	$4 \times 8 = 32$	$4 \times 9 = 36$	$4 \times 10 = 40$
$5 \times 6 = 30$	$5 \times 7 = 35$	$5 \times 8 = 40$	$5 \times 9 = 45$	$5 \times 10 = 50$
$6 \times 6 = 36$	$6 \times 7 = 42$	$6 \times 8 = 48$	$6 \times 9 = 54$	$6 \times 10 = 60$
$7 \times 6 = 42$	$7 \times 7 = 49$	$7 \times 8 = 56$	$7 \times 9 = 63$	$7 \times 10 = 70$
$8 \times 6 = 48$	$8 \times 7 = 56$	$8 \times 8 = 64$	$8 \times 9 = 72$	$8 \times 10 = 80$
$9 \times 6 = 54$	$9 \times 7 = 63$	$9 \times 8 = 72$	$9 \times 9 = 81$	$9 \times 10 = 90$
$10 \times 6 = 60$	$10 \times 7 = 70$	$10 \times 8 = 80$	$10 \times 9 = 90$	$10 \times 10 = 100$

Learn

To find the common multiples of two numbers, list the multiples of
each number. Find the numbers that appear in both lists.

Example

Find the common multiples of 6 and 8.

Multiples of 6: 6, 12, 18, (24) 30, 36, 42, (48) 54, 60
Multiples of 8: 8, 16, (24) 32, 40, (48) 56, 64, 72, 80

Common multiples: 24, 48

Lesson 5: **Odd and even numbers and multiples**

- Recognise odd and even numbers and multiples of 5, 10, 25, 50, 100 and 500 up to 1000
- Make general statements about odd and even numbers

Discover

Operation	Product
even × even	even
even × odd	even
odd × odd	odd

An even number multiplied by an even number gives an even number.

An even number multiplied by an odd number gives an even number.

An odd number multiplied by an odd number gives an odd number.

Learn

Divisibility rules help you work out if a number is a multiple of 5, 10, 25, 50, 100 or 500.

Multiple of	Rule
5	ends in 0 or 5
10	ends in 0
25	ends in 00, 25, 50 or 75
50	ends in 00 or 50
100	ends in 00
500	ends in 000 or 500

Example

What numbers will divide exactly into 250?

250 is divisible by 5, 10, 25 and 50 as the number ends in 50.

Lesson 6: **Comparing and ordering numbers**

- Order and compare positive and negative numbers to one million
- Use the >, < and = signs correctly

Discover

You can use place value to compare and order numbers.

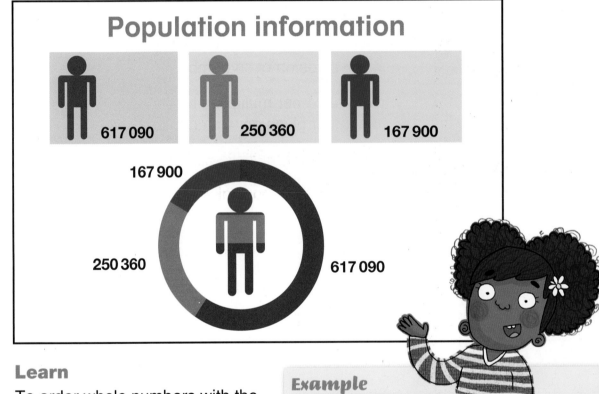

Population information

617 090   250 360   167 900

167 900

250 360

617 090

Learn

To order whole numbers with the same number of digits, begin by comparing the digits in the most significant place value position in both numbers.

The number with the largest-valued most significant digit is the larger number. If the digits are the same, compare the next most significant digits, then find which is larger.

Example

Compare and order the numbers 748 472, 732 836, 746 454 and 748 449.

HTh	TTh	Th	H	T	U
7	4	8	4	7	2
7	3	2	8	3	6
7	4	6	4	5	4
7	4	8	4	4	9

732 836 < 746 454 < 748 449 < 748 472

Lesson 7: **Rounding whole numbers**

- Round whole numbers to the nearest 10, 100 or 1000

Key words
- round
- rounding digit
- nearest 10
- nearest 100
- nearest 1000

Number

Discover

$437 209

Rounding is a useful tool, particularly in the financial world.

Learn

Think about the multiples of 10, 100 or 1000 before and after the number.

Look at the digit to the right of the rounding digit (the place value position you are rounding to). If it is:

- 5 or greater, round up
- less than 5, round down.

Include placeholder zeros as needed.

Example

Round 78 305 to the nearest 1000.

Method 1

78 305 is between 78 000 and 79 000. Which is the number closer to, 78 000 or 79 000?

Method 2

Look at the number to right of the 8, which is 3.

3 is less than 5, so round down to 78 000. Replace the rest of the digits with placeholder zeros.

Lesson 8: **Estimating**

- Make and justify estimates and approximations of large numbers
- Estimate where 4-digit numbers lie on an empty 0–10 000 line

Discover

To be able to make sensible estimates of a quantity it is important to have a **benchmark** figure, a number that is easy to calculate with, such as 10, 100 or 1000.

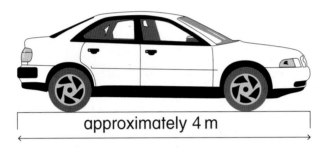

approximately 4 m

Learn

Benchmarks are known numbers of things that can be used to estimate the size of a larger group of things, like the number of jelly beans in a jar, or the population of a city.

Example
About how many pencil lengths might there be in a line 1 km long?

The average pencil is 20 cm in length. 1 km is 1000 × 100 cm = 100 000 cm. 100 000 ÷ 20 = 5000. So there might be 5000 pencils in a line 1 km long.

Lesson 1: **Revising whole numbers**

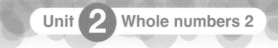

- Know what each digit represents in whole numbers up to 1 000 000
- Multiply and divide whole numbers by 10, 100 or 1000
- Round whole numbers to the nearest 10, 100 or 1000
- Order and compare positive and negative numbers
- Use the >, < and = signs correctly

Key words
- place value
- rounding
- order
- compare
- function
- function machine

Discover

In the real world, calculations rarely involve just a single step with only one operation.

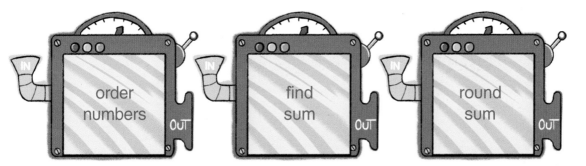

Learn

A function machine takes an input, applies a rule, such as a set of operations and delivers the answer as an output. A set of function machines can perform several operations on a number, for example: ordering, multiplying, dividing or rounding.

Example

Find the output of this machine for an input of 8373.

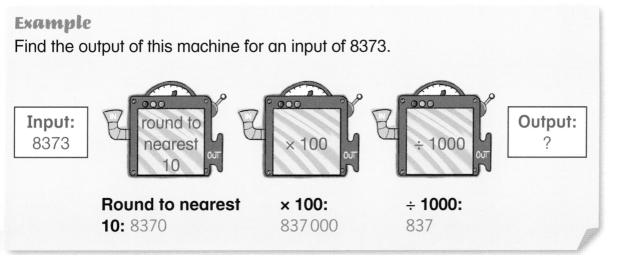

| Input: 8373 | round to nearest 10 | × 100 | ÷ 1000 | Output: ? |

Round to nearest 10: 8370   **× 100:** 837 000   **÷ 1000:** 837

Lesson 2: **Positive and negative numbers**

- Count on and back in repeated steps
- Order and compare positive and negative numbers
- Use the >, < and = signs correctly
- Recognise and extend number sequences

Key words
- negative number
- positive number
- step
- sequence
- count on
- count back

Discover

Saturday

-7/C°
-8°C

MAX | MIN

Sunday

4/C°
8°C

MAX | MIN

Monday

-3/C°
8°C

MAX | MIN

Learn

You can compare positive and negative numbers by thinking about their positions on the number line. Numbers to the right are greater than numbers to the left.

Example

Order the numbers: −13, 7, 13, −2, −7.

−15 −13 −10 −7 −5 −2 0 2 5 7 10 13 15

The number line shows that: −13 < −7 < −2 < 7 < 13

Lesson 3: **Factors, multiples and primes**

- Find factors of 2-digit numbers
- Find some common multiples of pairs of numbers
- Recognise prime numbers

Key words
- multiple
- factor
- prime
- composite

Number

Discover

When a number cannot be divided evenly by any number except 1 or itself it is called a **Prime number**.

Learn

A number is **prime** if it has only two factors: itself and 1.
Numbers that have more than two factors are **composite** numbers.
The number 1 only has one factor, so it is neither prime nor composite.

Example

Describe the numbers 22 and 19.

Factors of 22: 1, 2, 11, 22.
22 has more than two factors and so is **composite**.
Factors of 19: 1, 19.
19 has only two factors, 1 and 19, and so is **prime**.

Number

Lesson 4: **History of the number system**

- Recognise the historical origins of our number system and begin to understand how it developed
- Identify relationships between numbers using symbols and letters

🔍 **Key words**
- history
- number system
- variable
- expression

Discover

Throughout history there have been many important developments in mathematics.

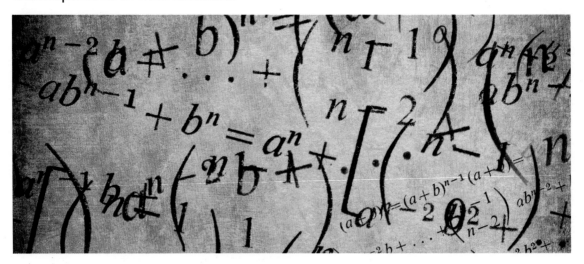

Learn

The Babylonians developed, a branch of mathematics known today as algebra. They found they could solve complex equations, mathematical statements where two things are expressed as being equal, by representing unknown numbers as letters or symbols.

The letter shows you that it doesn't matter what number you put in, the relationship between numbers and operations (add, multiply, divide, subtract) still exists.

Example

If n is 8, what is $2n - 7$?

If n represents any number then $2n - 7$ represents double the number subtract 7.
If n is 8, then $2n - 7$ is $(2 \times 8) - 7 = 9$

n	$2n - 7$
1	−5
2	−3
3	−1
4	1
5	3

Lesson 1: **Counting on and back in decimals (1)**

- Count on or back in decimal steps
- Recognise and extend number sequences

Key words
- place value
- decimal
- ones boundary
- tenths boundary

Discover

Counting money is easy. Just remember to count on or back in the same way as for decimals.

Learn

When counting in decimals, check what happens to the digits when the count crosses ones and tenths boundaries.

Crossing the ones boundary: the ones digit increases by 1; the tenths and hundredths digits reset to zero.

Crossing the tenths boundary: the tenths digit increases by 1; the hundredths digit resets to zero.

Example

Count on in steps of 0·3 from 2·3 to 3·5.

2·3, 2·6, 2·9, 3·2, 3·5

Count back in steps of 0·5 from 4·83 to 2·33.

4·83, 4·33, 3·83, 3·33, 2·83, 2·33

Lesson 2: **Place value in decimals (1)**

Number

- Know what each digit represents in 1- and 2-place decimal numbers
- Multiply and divide any whole number by 10, 100 or 1000 and explain the effect
- Multiply and divide decimals by 10 or 100

Key words
- place value
- decimal place

Discover

Being able to multiply or divide decimals by 10, 100 or 1000 is useful for converting between units of length, mass, capacity and money.

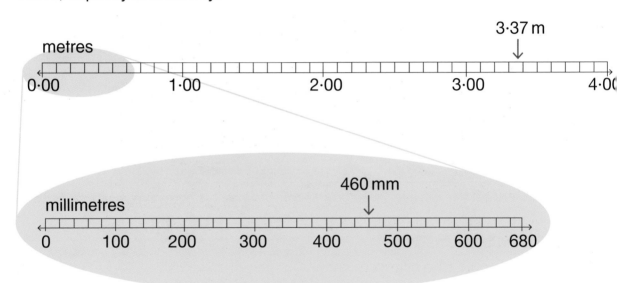

Learn

Multiply by 10, 100 or 1000: number becomes 10, 100 or 1000 times greater and the digits move 1, 2 or 3 places to the left.

Divide by 10, 100 or 1000: number becomes 10, 100 or 1000 times smaller and the digits move 1, 2 or 3 places to the right.

Example

What is 9·37 multiplied by 1000?

The digits move 3 places to the left, so: 9370

What is 4560 divided by 1000?

The digits move 3 places to the right, so: 4·56.

Lesson 3: **Comparing and ordering decimals (1)**

- Use the >, < and = signs correctly
- Order numbers with up to 2 decimal places

Key words
- compare
- order
- place value
- decimal place

Discover

Knowing how to order decimals is useful for working out which of several lengths is the longest.

7·1 m   7·74 m   7·47 m   7·7 m   6·9 m   7·3 m   7·43 m   7·34 m   7·83 m   7·22 m

Learn

To order decimals:

1. Write the numbers in a column, with the decimal points lined up.

2. If necessary, write one or more zeros to the right of the last digit, so that all the decimals have the same number of decimal digits.

3. Compare the digits in columns from left to right.

4. If the digits are the same move to the next column until a digit is greater.

5. Remove the 'largest' number from the list and record it.

6. Continue until the set of decimals are in order, largest to smallest.

7. For ascending order, swap around the order.

Example

Order largest to smallest: 3·87, 3·08, 3·84, 3·8

Write the decimals so they have the same number of digits:

3·87
3·08
3·84
3·80

Compare digits in columns from left to right. Write a number in brackets to denote order, 1 being the largest:

3·87 (1)
3·08 (4)
3·84 (2)
3·80 (3)

Reverse the order for smallest to largest: 3·08, 3·80, 3·84, 3·87.

Lesson 4: **Rounding decimals (1)**

• Round a number with 2 decimal places to the nearest tenth or to the nearest whole number

Number

Discover

Rounding is a key skill if you want to quickly estimate the total cost of several items.

Learn

To round decimals to the nearest tenth, look at the digit in the hundredths position.

• If it is 5 or greater: round up to the next tenth.
• If it is less than 5: the tenth remains the same.

Example

Round each number to the nearest tenth and whole number.

14·13 This rounds to 14·1 as the hundredths digit is less than 5.

9·45 This rounds to 9·5 as the hundredths digit is 5.

24·78 This rounds to 24·8 as the hundredths digit is greater than 5.

Lesson 1: **Counting on and back in decimals (2)**

Key words
- place value
- decimal
- ones boundary
- tenths boundary

- Count on or back in decimal steps
- Recognise and extend number sequences

Number

Discover
Counting in decimals is a useful skill.

0.05 0.10 0.15 0.20 0.25 0.30 0.35 0.40 0.45 0.50

Learn
Using the difference between one number and the next in a decimal number sequence will help you continue the sequence.

> **Example**
> What is the next number in the sequence?
> 2·88, 2·85, 2·82, 2·79, 2·76, ?
> Find the difference between the terms, for example:
> 2·88 − 2·85 = 0·03

Check whether the sequence is increasing or decreasing, then add or subtract the difference to the last number to find the next number in the sequence.

The sequence is decreasing so we need to subtract the difference from the last term.
2·76 − 0·03 = 2·73

The next number is 2·73.

17

Number

Lesson 2: **Place value in decimals (2)**

• Know what each digit represents in 1- and 2-place decimal numbers
• Multiply and divide any whole number by 10, 100 or 1000 and explain the effect
• Multiply and divide decimals by 10 or 100

Discover

Learn

You can combine amounts of liquid measured in different units by converting the amounts to the same unit using knowledge of multiplying and dividing by 10, 100 or 1000.

Example

Remember: 1 litre (*l*) = 1000 millilitres (ml)

What is 3·56 litres in millilitres?

Multiply by 1000 to convert to millilitres.
Move the digits 3 places to the left.

3·56 litres = 3560 ml

What is 780 millilitres in litres?

Divide by 1000 to convert to litres.
Move the digits 3 places to the right.

780 millilitres = 0·78 litres

Lesson 3: **Comparing and ordering decimals (2)**

Key words
- compare
- order
- place value
- decimal place

Number

- Use the >, < and = signs correctly
- Order numbers with up to 2 decimal places

Discover

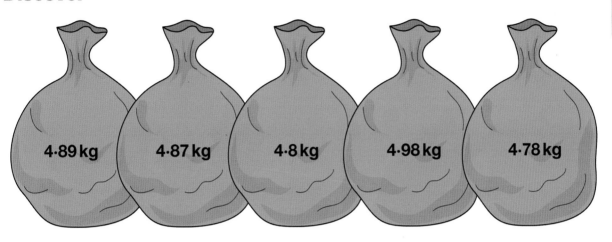

| 4·89 kg | 4·87 kg | 4·8 kg | 4·98 kg | 4·78 kg |

If you can order decimals, you can work out which of several measures is the greatest.

Learn

Remember what you have learned about ordering decimals in a previous lesson.

To order the sacks of vegetables above, write the decimals so they have the same number of digits:	Now compare them in columns from left to right. Put them in order with a number in brackets next to each one.
4.89	4.89 (2)
4.87	4.87 (3)
4.80	4.80 (4)
4.98	4.98 (1)
4.78	4.78 (5)

Another way you can show the order is by using the > and < signs.

4.89 > 4.87 > 4.80 < 4.98 > 4.78

Lesson 4: **Rounding decimals (2)**

- Round a number with 2 decimal places to the nearest tenth or to the nearest whole number

Key words
- round
- rounding digit
- decimal place

Discover

If several runners in a race finish close to each other, it could be useful to round their finishing times.

Learn

To round decimals to the next tenth, look at the digit in the hundredths position.

- If it is 5 or greater: round up to the next tenth.
- If it is less than 5: the tenth remains the same.

Example

Round each number to the nearest tenth.

17·24   This rounds to 17·2 as the hundredths digit is less than 5.

12·75   This rounds to 12·8 as the hundredths digit is 5.

15·88   This rounds to 15·9 as the hundredths digit is greater than 5.

Lesson 1: **Counting on and back in fractions**

📌 **Key words**
• **halves**
• **thirds**
• **quarters**
• **fifths**
• **exchange**

• Counting on and back in fractions, such as thirds

Discover

Counting in fractions is like counting in whole numbers, but with mixed numbers.

$\frac{1}{2}$, 1, $1\frac{1}{2}$, 2, $2\frac{1}{2}$, 3, $3\frac{1}{2}$, 4

$\frac{1}{2}$ 1 $1\frac{1}{2}$ 2 $2\frac{1}{2}$ 3 $3\frac{1}{2}$ 4

Learn

When counting in fractions, you must think how the number changes when it crosses a whole number boundary.

Every time the fractional part of the number makes a whole number, the ones digit increases by 1 and the next fraction has 1 as the numerator.

Example

$\frac{1}{5}, \frac{2}{5}, \frac{3}{5}, \frac{4}{5}$ … What is the next number in the sequence?

The next number is $\frac{5}{5}$ or 1.

The number after that will be $1\frac{1}{5}$.

Lesson 2: **Equivalent fractions**

- Recognise equivalence between fractions

Discover

Equivalent fractions are different ways of showing the same fraction of the whole.

Learn

You can make equivalent fractions by multiplying or dividing the numerator and denominator by the same number.

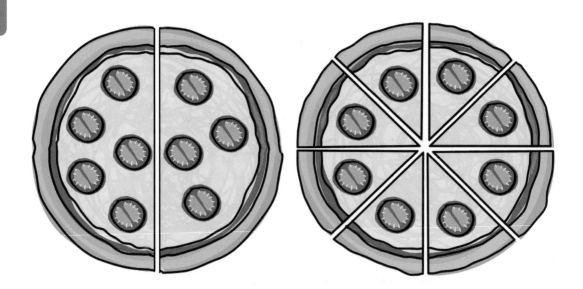

Example

What are equivalent fractions of $\frac{1}{3}$?

$$\frac{1}{3} \;\overset{\times 2}{\underset{\times 2}{=}}\; \frac{2}{6} \;\overset{\times 3}{\underset{\times 3}{=}}\; \frac{6}{18} \;\overset{\times 10}{\underset{\times 10}{=}}\; \frac{60}{180}$$

$$\frac{1}{3} \;\overset{\times 3}{\underset{\times 3}{=}}\; \frac{3}{9} \qquad \frac{1}{3} \;\overset{\times 5}{\underset{\times 5}{=}}\; \frac{5}{15}$$

Lesson 3: **Comparing fractions**

Key words
- **compare**
- **equivalent fraction**
- **numerator**
- **denominator**

- Compare fractions with the same denominator and related denominators

Number

Discover

You can use a fraction wall to compare fractions with different denominators.

1							
$\frac{1}{4}$		$\frac{1}{4}$		$\frac{1}{4}$		$\frac{1}{4}$	
$\frac{1}{8}$	$\frac{1}{8}$	$\frac{1}{8}$	$\frac{1}{8}$	$\frac{1}{8}$	$\frac{1}{8}$	$\frac{1}{8}$	$\frac{1}{8}$

Learn

From the fraction wall, you can see that $\frac{3}{4}$ and $\frac{6}{8}$ take up the same amount of the whole and therefore are equivalent: $\frac{3}{4} = \frac{6}{8}$.

What about $\frac{7}{8}$ and $\frac{3}{4}$? You can use equivalent fractions to rename fractions so that you can compare them. You know that $\frac{7}{8}$ is the greater fraction because $\frac{3}{4}$ is equivalent to $\frac{6}{8}$ and $\frac{7}{8} > \frac{6}{8}$.

Example
Which is greater, $\frac{2}{3}$ or $\frac{5}{6}$?

$\frac{2}{3}$ is equivalent to $\frac{4}{6}$

$\frac{4}{6} < \frac{5}{6}$ so $\frac{2}{3} < \frac{5}{6}$.

Lesson 4: **Fraction and decimal equivalents**

- Begin to recognise and use the equivalence between fractions and decimals

Key words
- equivalent
- fraction
- decimal
- tenths
- hundredths
- quarters

Discover

It is useful to be able to convert one kind of number into another. For example, it is easier to add the measures $\frac{2}{5}$ kilogram and 0·5 kilogram if you convert $\frac{2}{5}$ to a decimal.

0·5 kg

$\frac{2}{5}$ **kg**

Learn

0·5 is equivalent to $\frac{5}{10}$ or $\frac{1}{2}$.

0·25 is equivalent to $\frac{25}{100}$ or $\frac{1}{4}$.

0·1 is equivalent to $\frac{1}{10}$.

0·75 is equivalent to $\frac{75}{100}$ or $\frac{3}{4}$.

Example
Work out $\frac{4}{5}$ + 0·5

Convert $\frac{4}{5}$ to 0·8 by thinking of it as a division calculation. $4 \div 5 = 0.8$

$0.8 + 0.5 = 1.3$

Lesson 5: **Ordering mixed numbers**

Key words
• fraction
• decimal

Number

• Order mixed numbers and place them between whole numbers on a number line

Discover

Sometimes you need to add mixed numbers together. For example, a café may need to count up whole and fractional amounts of cakes.

Learn

To order mixed numbers you can make them into equivalent fractions, so they all have the same denominator, or you can convert them to decimals.

Example

Order the numbers smallest to largest: $7\frac{1}{5}$, $6\frac{4}{5}$, $7\frac{1}{2}$, $6\frac{7}{10}$, $7\frac{3}{5}$.

Convert to equivalent fractions – tenths. $7\frac{2}{10}$, $6\frac{8}{10}$, $7\frac{5}{10}$, $6\frac{7}{10}$, $7\frac{6}{10}$.

Then order them on a number line:

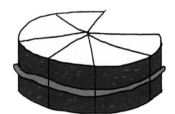

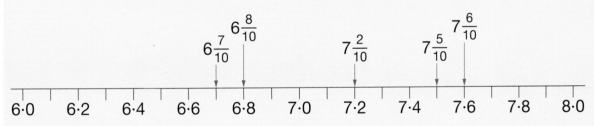

Convert to decimals: 7·2, 6·8, 7·5, 6·7, 7·6.

Position the decimals on the number line:

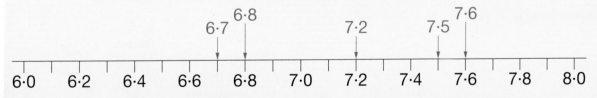

Decimal order is 6·7, 6·8, 7·25, 7·5, 7·6, so mixed number order will be:

$6\frac{7}{10}$, $6\frac{4}{5}$, $7\frac{1}{4}$, $7\frac{1}{2}$, $7\frac{3}{5}$.

Lesson 6: **Improper fractions and mixed numbers**

Key words
- improper fraction
- mixed number

• Convert an improper fraction to a mixed number

Discover

In an improper fraction, the **numerator** (top number) is greater than or equal to the **denominator** (bottom number).

$$\frac{12}{5} = 2\frac{2}{5}$$

Learn

A visual model can help convert improper fractions to mixed numbers.

Here is a circle model for the fraction $\frac{24}{5}$.

 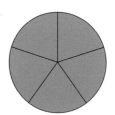 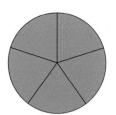  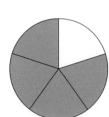

Think visually!

$$\frac{24}{5} = \frac{5}{5} + \frac{5}{5} + \frac{5}{5} + \frac{5}{5} + \frac{4}{5} = 4\frac{4}{5}$$

Lesson 7: **Reducing fractions**

- Reduce fractions to their simplest form

Key word
- reduce (simplify)
- highest common factor (HCF)

Discover

Reducing a fraction, by finding the highest common factor, makes it easier to understand.
This illustration shows $\frac{66}{88}$.

1	2	3	4	5	6	7	8	9	10
11	12	13	14	15	16	17	18	19	20
21	22	23	24	25	26	27	28	29	30
31	32	33	34	35	36	37	38	39	40
41	42	43	44	45	46	47	48	49	50
51	52	53	54	55	56	57	58	59	60
61	62	63	64	65	66	67	68	69	70
71	72	73	74	75	76	77	78	79	80
81	82	83	84	85	86	87	88		

Learn

To reduce a fraction, you divide the numerator and the denominator by the highest common factor of both numbers.

Example

Write the fraction $\frac{16}{40}$ in its simplest form.

Factors of 16:   1, 2, 4, 8, 16

Factors of 40:   1, 2, 4, 5, 8, 10, 20, 40

Common factors of 16 and 40:   1, 2, 4, 8.

Highest common factor is 8.

Divide numerator and denominator by 8:

$$\frac{16}{40} = \frac{16 \div 8}{40 \div 8} = \frac{2}{5}$$

$\frac{16}{40}$ in its simplest form is $\frac{2}{5}$.

Lesson 8: **Decimal fractions**

Key word
• decimal fraction

• Begin to use division to convert a common fraction to a decimal fraction

Discover

To find the decimal equivalent of a fraction you use division. For example, the decimal equivalent of the fraction $\frac{3}{4}$ is 0·75 as $3 \div 4 = 0.75$.

$$\frac{3}{4} \rightarrow 3 \div 4$$

$$\frac{3}{4} = 0.75$$

Learn

You can think of a fraction such as $\frac{1}{8}$ as a division calculation: 1 divided by 8. The answer to a division is usually expressed as a decimal fraction, so that: $\frac{1}{8} = 0.125$

Example

Write the fraction $\frac{5}{16}$ as a decimal fraction.

Consider the fraction as a division and use a calculator to solve it: $5 \div 16 = 0.3125$

Lesson 1: **What is a percentage?**

- Understand percentage as 'the number of parts in every hundred'

Key words
- percent (%)
- percentage
- hundredths

Number

Discover

A percentage is a fraction out of 100.

Percentages tell you the number of parts in every hundred.

Learn

Per cent means 'in every hundred'. The sign for per cent is %.

In the picture above, there are 100 cones. Three cones are red and the rest are blue. To describe the red cones you could say three hundredths ($\frac{3}{100}$) or you could express them as a percentage: 3 per cent, or 3%.

For 7 cones in every 100, you write 7%; for 29 cones in every 100, you write 29%.

Example

73 cones out of 100 are red. How do you write this as a percentage?

73 in 100 can be written as $\frac{73}{100}$ or 73%. The percentage sign (%) indicates a percentage, a number expressed as a fraction of 100.

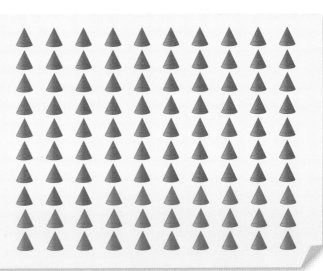

Lesson 2: **Fractions as percentages**

- Express $\frac{1}{2}$, $\frac{1}{4}$, $\frac{1}{3}$, $\frac{1}{10}$, $\frac{1}{100}$, and multiples of tenths as percentages

Key words
- percent (%)
- percentage
- hundredths

Discover

It is easier to compare percentages than fractions. If you convert the fractions to percentages on these reduced items you can see that the second shop offers the biggest discount: 10%, 50%, 25%.

$\frac{1}{10}$ off $\frac{1}{2}$ off $\frac{1}{4}$ off

Learn

It can be easier to see which is bigger and which is smaller if you look at percentages, rather than fractions.

Fraction	$\frac{1}{2}$	$\frac{1}{3}$	$\frac{1}{4}$	$\frac{1}{10}$	$\frac{1}{100}$
Percentage	50%	33·3%	25%	10%	1%

Example

What is $\frac{1}{4}$ as a percentage?

To write the fraction as a percentage, you need to have a denominator of 100.

If you scale up the fraction by a factor of 25, you will have $25 \times 4 = 100$ as the denominator and 25 as the numerator.

Number

Lesson 3: **Percentages of shapes and whole numbers**

🔴 **Key words**
* percent (%)
* percentage
* fraction

- Find simple percentages of shapes and whole numbers

Discover

A fact web is a useful way to organise and make links between the calculations involved when finding percentages of an amount.

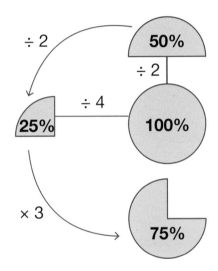

Learn

You can use one percentage to find another.

This fact web shows percentages of the amount $1600. To calculate 75% of the amount, find 25% and multiply it by three.

100% is $1600.

50% is $800   ($1600 ÷ 2)

25% is $400   ($1600 ÷ 4 or $800 ÷ 2)

75% is $1200   ($400 × 3)

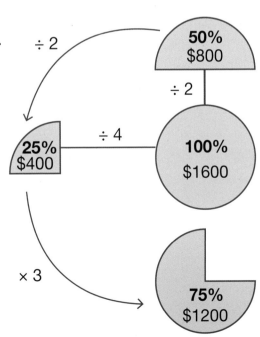

31

Number

Lesson 4: **Problems involving percentages**

- Solve problems that involve finding simple percentages of whole numbers

Key words
- percent (%)
- percentage
- fraction

Discover

1%	1%	1%	1%	1%	1%	1%	1%	1%	1%
1%	1%	1%	1%	1%	1%	1%	1%	1%	1%
1%	1%	1%	1%	1%	1%	1%	1%	1%	1%
1%	1%	1%	1%	1%	1%	1%	1%	1%	1%
1%	1%	1%	1%	1%	1%	1%	1%	1%	1%
1%	1%	1%	1%	1%	1%	1%	1%	1%	1%
1%	1%	1%	1%	1%	1%	1%	1%	1%	1%
1%	1%	1%	1%	1%	1%	1%	1%	1%	1%
1%	1%	1%	1%	1%	1%	1%	1%	1%	1%
1%	1%	1%	1%	1%	1%	1%	1%	1%	1%

We calculate 1% of an amount by finding one hundredth (or dividing by 100).

Learn

You can build larger percentages from smaller percentages.

You can use 1% to find 2%, 3% … and then you add these to 10%, 20% … to calculate other percentages, such as 11% and 23%.

The grid shows that if you know 1% of 500 is 5 you can calculate any percentage of 500. For example, 13% is 65.

5	5	5	5	5	5	5	5	5	5
5	5	5	5	5	5	5	5	5	5
5	5	5	5	5	5	5	5	5	5
5	5	5	5	5	5	5	5	5	5
5	5	5	5	5	5	5	5	5	5
5	5	5	5	5	5	5	5	5	5
5	5	5	5	5	5	5	5	5	5
5	5	5	5	5	5	5	5	5	5
5	5	5	5	5	5	5	5	5	5
5	5	5	5	5	5	5	5	5	5

Example

What is 23% of $2600?

10% of $2600 is $260 ($2600 ÷ 10)

20% of $2600 is $520

(2 × $260 (10%))

1% of $2600 is $26

($2600 ÷ 100)

23% of $2600 = 20% + 3% = $520 + (3 × $26 (1%)) =

$520 + $78 = $598

$26	$26	$26	$26	$26	$26	$26	$26	$26	$26
$26	$26	$26	$26	$26	$26	$26	$26	$26	$26
$26	$26	$26	$26	$26	$26	$26	$26	$26	$26
$26	$26	$26	$26	$26	$26	$26	$26	$26	$26
$26	$26	$26	$26	$26	$26	$26	$26	$26	$26
$26	$26	$26	$26	$26	$26	$26	$26	$26	$26
$26	$26	$26	$26	$26	$26	$26	$26	$26	$26
$26	$26	$26	$26	$26	$26	$26	$26	$26	$26
$26	$26	$26	$26	$26	$26	$26	$26	$26	$26
$26	$26	$26	$26	$26	$26	$26	$26	$26	$26

Lesson 1: **Ratio**

- Understand ratio as comparing part to part

Number

Discover

Look at the way each child is decorating their cake.

Learn

Ratio is a way to compare one number or quantity with another.

When we use ratio, we compare <u>part</u> of something with another <u>part</u>.

Example

The ratio of apples to pears is **3 apples for every 1 pear** or **3 to 1**.

Part   Part

The ratio of blue to orange counters is **2 blue counters for every 4 orange counters** or **2 to 4**.

Part   Part

The ratio of orange to blue counters is **4 orange counters for every 2 blue counters** or **4 to 2**.

Number

Lesson 2: **Ratio problems**

- Solve problems that involve ratio

Discover

What is the difference between these orange drinks?

How could you make the same strength drinks in glasses that were twice the size?

1 part orange juice, 5 parts water.

1 part orange juice, 2 parts water.

Learn

If we know a ratio, we can still use it even when the quantities increase.

This shows a ratio of red to blue of 1 to 3.

The number of counters has doubled, but the ratio of red to blue is still the same. 2 : 6 is equivalent to 1 : 3.

Example

How many eggs will be needed to make a cake large enough for 10 people?

Cake recipe:
Serves 5 people
You will need: 2 eggs.

The ratio of eggs to people is 2 eggs for every 5 people.

If the number of people doubles, the number of eggs needs to double too.

The amounts have changed, but the ratio is still the same.

4 eggs are needed to serve 10 people.

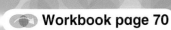
Lesson 3: **Proportion**

- Understand proportion as comparing part to whole

Key words
- compare
- proportion
- out of
- fraction
- whole
- part
- equivalent

Number

Discover

Who is better at basketball? Why?

Learn

Proportion is a way to show a number or quantity as part of the whole amount. We can write this as a fraction.

Example

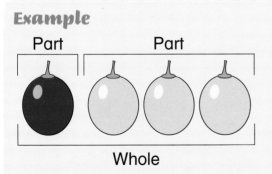

Part   Part

Whole

Proportion is different than ratio.

The ratio of red to green grapes is 1 to 3.

The proportion of red grapes to the whole is $\frac{1}{4}$.

The proportion of green grapes to the whole is $\frac{3}{4}$.

Lesson 4: **Proportion problems**

Key words
* compare
* direct proportion
* out of
* fraction
* whole
* part
* equivalent

• Solve problems that involve direct proportion

Discover

How large should the elephant be in the second picture? Why?

Learn

We can use proportions to help work out quantities.

If we know the **whole amount** and the proportion, we can work out what the **part** is.

What is $\frac{1}{2}$ of 24 cm?

If we know the **part** and the proportion, we can work out what the whole amount is.

A picture of a mouse is 2 cm tall. Mice are $\frac{1}{30}$ of the height of elephants. To keep the proportion correct, how tall should the picture of an elephant be?

Example

Alisha is making a necklace.

For every 1 plastic bead she uses 4 wooden beads.

The ratio of plastic to wooden beads is 1 : 4.

The proportion of plastic beads is $\frac{1}{5}$.

If she uses 15 beads altogether, how many will be plastic?

We know that $\frac{1}{5}$ are plastic.

$15 \div 5 = 3$.

So, 3 beads will be plastic.

Lesson 1: **Mental addition (1)**

- Use place value and number facts to add 2-digit numbers and to add 3-digit multiples of 10

Key words
- addition
- jottings
- partitioning
- bridging

Discover

Mental addition is adding numbers 'in your head'.

$37 + $48 = ?

Learn

A good strategy for mentally adding numbers is to split or partition them by place value and add the parts together, in stages. You can use empty number lines and other jottings to support the calculation.

Example

There are different ways to split and regroup the numbers by place value.

37 + 48

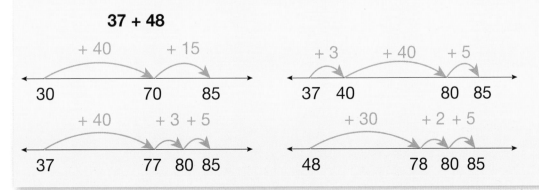

Number

Lesson 2: **Written addition (1)**

- Add numbers with the same or different numbers of digits

Discover

As numbers become too large to calculate mentally, you need to use a written strategy to solve the calculation.

Numbers are lined up in columns according to place value. The numbers in the columns are added separately and recombined to find the answer.

$$
\begin{array}{ccc}
\text{H} & \text{T} & \text{U} \\
5 & 6 & 7 \\
+ \quad 3 & 2 & 9 \\
\hline
\\
\hline
\end{array}
$$

Learn

To solve an addition calculation, you can use a written strategy, for example, the expanded written method, or the formal written method, which sometimes requires digits to be carried over to the next place value column.

Example

To add 548 + 387:

Expanded written method   Leading to: Formal written method

$$
\begin{array}{r}
5\ 4\ 8 \\
+\ 3\ 8\ 7 \\
\hline
1\ 5 \\
1\ 2\ 0 \\
8\ 0\ 0 \\
\hline
9\ 3\ 5 \\
\end{array}
\qquad
\begin{array}{r}
5\ 4\ 8 \\
+\ 3\ 8\ 7 \\
\hline
9\ 3\ 5 \\
\scriptstyle 1\ \ \ 1 \\
\end{array}
$$

Lesson 3: **Mental subtraction (1)**

🔍 **Key words**
• **subtraction**
• **jottings**
• **partitioning**

- Use place value and number facts to subtract 2-digit numbers and to subtract 3-digit multiples of 10

Number

Discover

You can take away numbers 'in your head'. This is mental subtraction.

Davinder has $770 to spend. He wants a game console that costs $490. He wants to know how much he will have left.

He knows he can split numbers by place value and subtract the separate places. He writes down:

$770 - 490 = (700 - 400) + (70 - 90)$

The second subtraction gives a negative number. Is there a better strategy?

SAVINGS ACCOUNT

$770

$490

Learn

A good strategy for mentally subtracting numbers is to split or partition the second number by place value and subtract the hundreds, the tens and the units. You can use blank number lines to help you.

Example

To work out 79 subtract 33, partition 33 into 30 and 3 and subtract in smaller or larger steps of ten and units.

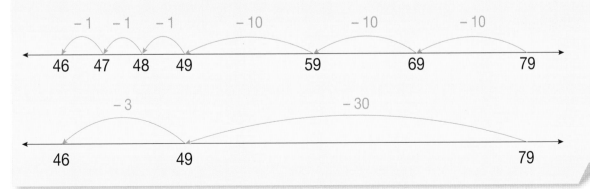

Number

Lesson 4: **Written subtraction (1)**

* Subtract numbers with the same or different numbers of digits

Discover

Some subtraction calculations are too difficult to work out mentally, so partitioning or exchanging can help.

$$\begin{array}{r} 5\ 6\ 6 \\ -\ 2\ 2\ 8 \\ \hline \end{array}$$

Instead of splitting the numbers according to their place value …

$566 = 500 + 60 + 6$.

$228 = 200 + 20 + 8$

… you can split them to make the calculation easier.

$566 = 550 + 16$

$228 = 220 + 8$

550 − 220 = 230 and
16 − 8 = 8.
The answer is 238!

Learn

If you use a written strategy, you might need to split the numbers in a similar way, exchanging 1 ten for 10 units. This is called renaming or decomposition.

$$\begin{array}{r} 5\ ^5\!6\ ^1\!6 \\ -\ 2\ 2\ 8 \\ \hline 8 \end{array}$$

Example

Use partitioning or a written method to work out 782 − 467.

Partitioning

$$\begin{array}{r} 770 + 12 \\ -\ 460 + 7 \\ \hline 310 + 5 \\ = 315 \end{array}$$

Expanded written method

$$\begin{array}{r} 700 \quad \overset{70}{\cancel{80}} \quad \overset{12}{\cancel{2}} \\ -\quad 400 \quad 60 \quad 7 \\ \hline 300 + 10 + 5 \end{array}$$

Formal written method

$$\begin{array}{r} 7\ ^7\!8\ ^1\!2 \\ -\ \ 4\ 6\ 7 \\ \hline 3\ 1\ 5 \end{array}$$

Lesson 1: **Decimals totalling 1 or 10**

- Recall pairs of decimals that total 1 and 10

Key word
- decimal pair

Number

Discover

Knowing how to find decimal pairs that add to make 1 is useful.

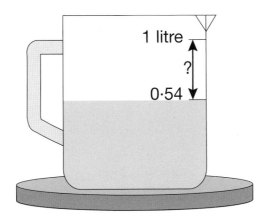

Learn

The digits of one-place decimals that total 10 are the same as those of whole numbers that total 100, but they are 10 times smaller.

Example

Find the missing numbers.

$6.7 + \boxed{} = 10$

You know that
$67 + 33$ is 100, so you also know that
$6.7 + 3.3$ is 10 and
$0.67 + 0.33$ is 1.
Therefore the missing numbers are 3.3 and 0.33.

The digits of two-place decimals that total 1 are the same as those of whole numbers that total 100, but they are 100 times smaller.

Example

Find the missing numbers.

$0.67 + \boxed{} = 1$

41

Lesson 2: **Adding decimals mentally**

- Use a range of mental strategies to add pairs of decimals

Key words
- tenths
- hundredths
- place value
- partitioning

Discover

Adding decimal numbers mentally is like adding whole numbers, but you need to use place value and knowledge of decimals to adjust for the difference in place value.

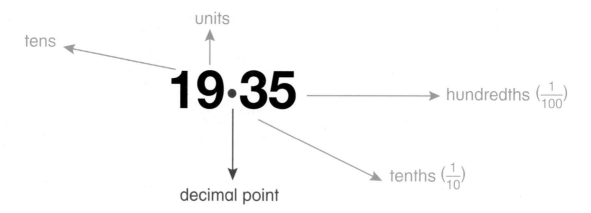

units

tens

19·35

hundredths ($\frac{1}{100}$)

decimal point

tenths ($\frac{1}{10}$)

Learn

When adding decimals, you can partition the whole number and decimal parts, add the parts, then combine.

Example

$$4·8 + 3·7 = 4 + 0.8 + 3 + 0.7$$
$$= (4 + 3) + (0·8 + 0·7)$$
$$= 7 + 1·5$$
$$= 8·5$$

or

$$4·8 + 3·7 = 4·8 + 3 + 0·7$$
$$= 7·8 + 0.7$$
$$= 8·5$$

Lesson 3: **Adding near multiples**

Key words
* place value
* jottings
* compensation

* Add a near multiple of 10, 100 or 1000
* Add a near multiple of 1 when adding decimals

Discover

Prices of items in shops often end in an amount such as 99 cents.
Suppose a gift shop sells two items priced $11.76 and $12.99.
How would you use rounding and adjusting to add the prices?

Learn

To use the compensation strategy, round one number to simplify the calculation then adjust the answer to compensate for the original change.

Example

$16.64 + $15.97 =

Round $15.97 to $16. Then subtract $0.03 to adjust for adding 3 cents too many.

16·64 + 15·97 = (16·64 + 16) − 0·03

= 32·64 − 0·03

= 32·61

The answer is $32.61.

43

Lesson 4: **Written addition of decimals**

• Add numbers with the same or different numbers of decimal places

Discover

When using a written method to add decimals it is important to remember to line up the numbers according to their place value.

$$
\begin{array}{r}
3\cdot 5 \\
0\cdot 5 \\
+ \\
\hline
4\cdot 0
\end{array}
$$

Learn

Column addition for decimals is similar to that for whole numbers.

Add the digits in each place value column.

Make sure all the decimal points are lined up and the answer has the decimal point in the right place.

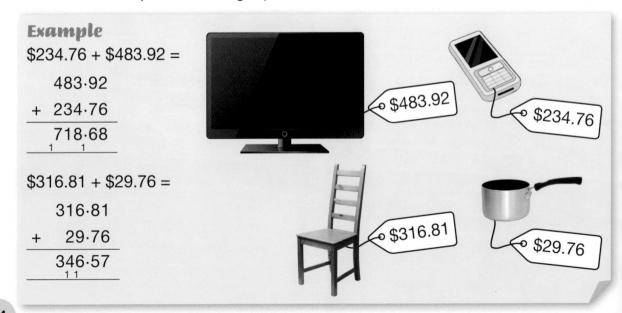

Example
$234.76 + $483.92 =

$$
\begin{array}{r}
483\cdot 92 \\
+ 234\cdot 76 \\
\hline
718\cdot 68 \\
_{1}_{1}
\end{array}
$$

$316.81 + $29.76 =

$$
\begin{array}{r}
316\cdot 81 \\
+ 29\cdot 76 \\
\hline
346\cdot 57 \\
_{1\,1}
\end{array}
$$

$483.92

$234.76

$316.81

$29.76

Lesson 5: **Subtracting decimals mentally**

- Use a range of mental strategies to subtract pairs of decimals

Number

Discover

$$78 - 25 = 53$$
$$7{\cdot}8 - 2{\cdot}5 = 5{\cdot}3$$

Subtracting decimal numbers mentally is like subtracting whole numbers. You just need to use place value and knowledge of decimals to adjust for the difference in place value.

Learn

You can use partitioning as a mental strategy for subtraction. Split the second number into its whole number and decimal parts. Subtract the whole number first, then the decimal part.

Example

$8{\cdot}2 - 5{\cdot}9 =$

$$8{\cdot}2 - 5{\cdot}9 = 8{\cdot}2 - 5 - 0{\cdot}9$$
$$= 3{\cdot}2 - 0{\cdot}9$$
$$= 2{\cdot}3$$

Lesson 6: **Subtracting near multiples**

- Subtract a near multiple of 10, 100 or 1000
- Subtract mentally near multiples of one with one decimal place

> **Key words**
> - place value
> - bridging
> - jottings
> - compensation

Discover

A ring is on sale in a jewellery shop for $7700. Then the price is reduced by $1999. How would you use rounding and adjusting to find the reduced price of the ring?

JEWELLERY PALACE

BUY IN STORE & ONLINE

$1999 OFF*

WHILE STOCKS LAST

* NORMAL PRICE: $7700

Learn

To use the compensation strategy for subtraction, you round the second number to simplify the calculation then adjust the answer to compensate for the original change.

> **Example**
> $74.13 – $39.98
> $74{\cdot}13 - 39{\cdot}98 = (74{\cdot}13 - 40) + 0{\cdot}02$
> $\qquad\qquad = 34{\cdot}13 + 0{\cdot}02$
> $\qquad\qquad = 34{\cdot}15$
> The answer is $34.15.

Lesson 7: **Written subtraction of decimals**

- Subtract numbers with the same or different numbers of decimal places

Discover

When using a written method to subtract decimals, remember to line up the numbers according to their place value. What is wrong with this layout?

$$\begin{array}{r} 162\cdot49 \\ -\ 641\cdot75 \\ \hline \\ \hline \end{array}$$

$641.75

$162.49 off!

Learn

To subtract a smaller decimal number from a larger decimal number, write the larger number above the smaller number with the decimal points lined up.

Then calculate the subtraction as you would for whole numbers and line up the decimal point in the answer.

Example

Find the difference between the price of the two toys.

$63·74 – $37·27 =

$$\begin{array}{r} {}^{5\,1}\ {}^{6\,1}\quad \\ 63\cdot\cancel{7}4 \\ -\ 37\cdot27 \\ \hline 26\cdot47 \end{array}$$

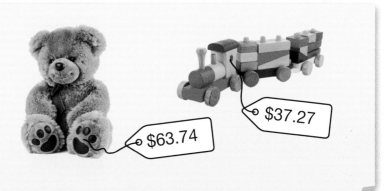

$37.27

$63.74

Number

Lesson 8: **Positive and negative numbers**

- Find the difference between positive and negative numbers, and between two negative numbers

Discover

When the temperature is high, you feel hot.
When the temperature is low, you feel cool.
When the temperature is a negative number, you feel very cold.

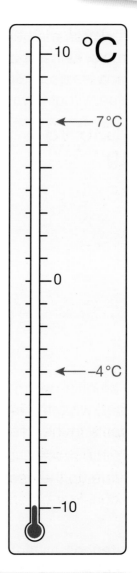

Learn

To work out the difference between a positive and a negative temperature, you must work out the difference between the positive value and 0°C, then the difference between 0°C and the negative value, and then add these two numbers together.

Example

To find the difference between 12°C and −9°C:

- the difference between −9°C and 0°C is 9 degrees
- the difference between 0°C and 12°C is 12 degrees
- add 9 and 12: the difference in temperature is 21 degrees.

Lesson 1: **Mental addition (2)**

- Use a range of mental strategies to add whole numbers and decimals

Key words
- decimal pair
- place value
- partitioning
- compensation
- rounding

Discover

The more confident you are with addition, the faster you can choose the most efficient strategy to solve a problem.

Kamila needs to add the prices of the two items she has bought. She needs to choose a strategy to do this.

$35.98

$43.70

Learn

The best strategy to use depends on:

- the numbers involved – different methods work better with certain numbers
- your preferences – use a strategy you feel comfortable with but consider others that may be more efficient.

Example

To add 480 and 390, add a near multiple of 100:

480 + 400 then adjust by subtracting 10:

480 + 400 = 880, then subtract 10,
880 − 10 = 870.

Lesson 2: **Written addition (2)**

- Use a written method to add whole numbers and decimals

Key words
- place value
- estimate
- expanded written method
- formal written method
- decimal point
- carry

Discover

Annamaria is shopping online and wants to buy two items priced $473 and $292. She uses a pencil and paper to work out the total cost of the two items. Which written methods could she use?

$473

$292

Learn

The column method of addition is a good written strategy for adding numbers.

Line up the numbers below each other so that the same place values are in one column. Add the numbers in each column beginning on the right (lowest place value) and working left.

When one place value column becomes two digits you need to carry (regroup) that number over into the next column.

Example

Expanded written method

```
     473
+    292
       5
     160
     600
     765
```

Formal written method

```
     473
+    292
     765
     1
```

50

Lesson 3: **Mental subtraction (2)**

- Use a range of mental strategies to subtract whole numbers and decimals

Number

Discover

George needs to find the distance he has left to run after completing 670 metres of a 930 metre long track. Which method should he use?

270 m

?

400 m

Learn

Although it's always a good idea to use a method you are familiar with, it is important to know how to use other subtraction strategies just in case one is better suited to solving the problem.

> **Example**
> To subtract 2497 from 6754:
> - round 2497 to 2500
> - then add 3 to adjust for subtracting 3 too many.
>
> $6754 - 2497 = 6754 - 2500 + 3 = 4254 + 3 = 4257$
>
>
>
> The answer is 4257.

Lesson 4: **Written subtraction (2)**

Key words
• place value
• estimate
• rename (decompose)

- Use a written method to subtract whole numbers and decimals

Discover

Pierre has saved $83.72 and wants to buy a computer game for $36.49. He uses a pencil and paper to work out how much he will have left after buying the game. Which written methods could he use?

$36.49

$83.72

Learn

The column method of subtraction is a good written strategy for subtracting numbers.

Line up the numbers below each other so the same place values are in one column. Begin subtracting on the right (lowest place value) and work left.

To subtract a larger number from a smaller number you need to use renaming. Renaming involves taking value from one place and giving it to another.

Example
$83.72 − $36.49

$$\begin{array}{r} {}^{7}\,{}^{13}\quad{}^{6}\,{}^{12} \\ 8\cancel{3}\cdot\cancel{7}\cancel{2} \\ -\ 36\cdot49 \\ \hline 47\cdot23 \end{array}$$

Lesson 1: **Multiplying multiples of 10 and 100**

Number

- Multiply pairs of multiples of 10 or multiples of 10 and 100

Discover

What is the combined mass of 60 tubs each with a mass of 390 g?

To estimate the answer, round 390 to 400 and multiply by 60.

You know 4×6 is 24, so 400×60 is 24 000.

You can use this estimate to check the answer.

Quantity	Item description
60	Face Cream (390 g)

Face Cream

390 grams

Learn

- To multiply pairs of multiples of 10: find the product of a related number fact for multiplying a single-digit number by a single-digit number, then multiply by 100.
- To multiply multiples of 10 by multiples of 100: find the product of a related number fact for multiplying a single-digit number by a single-digit number, then multiply by 1000.

Example

To multiply 30×700, solve a related problem: 3×7 (or 30×7) then adjust for place value.

$$3 \times 7 = 21$$
$$30 \times 700 = 21 \times 1000$$
$$= 21\ 000$$

53

Lesson 2: **Multiplying near multiples of 10**

- Multiply near multiples of 10 by multiplying by the multiple of 10 and adjusting

Key words
- multiply by
- compensation
- round
- adjust

Discover

Samira wants to buy 19 DVDs priced at $24 each. She thinks:

If I were to buy 20 DVDs rather than 19, the price would be $24 × 20.

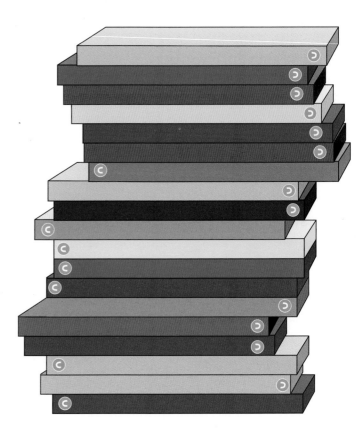

But she only wants 19 DVDs. How should Samira adjust this figure?

Learn

To multiply a number by a near multiple of 10, round the number that you are multiplying by to a multiple of 10 and then adjust for multiplying by too few or too many.

Example

$53 \times 28 = 53 \times 30 - (53 \times 2)$	$46 \times 61 = 46 \times 60 + (46 \times 1)$
$= 1590 - 106$	$= 2760 + 46$
$= 1484$	$= 2806$

Number

Lesson 3: **Multiplying by halving and doubling**

* Multiply by halving one number and doubling the other

Discover

Marie baked 8 trays of cakes. Each tray holds 36 cakes. How many cakes has she baked?

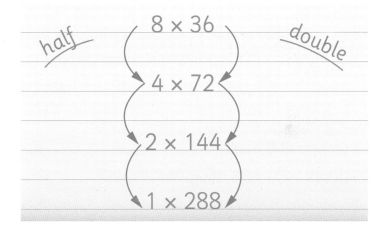

8×36 — half / double

4×72

2×144

1×288

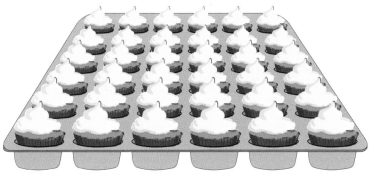

Learn

It is useful to know how to double and halve numbers when you need to multiply.

If one of the numbers you are multiplying is even, you can halve that number and double the other, then multiply. You can keep doing this until the multiplication is easier to solve.

Example

$35 \times 16 =$

$35 \times 16 = 70 \times 8$

$\qquad = 560$

$15 \times 32 =$

$15 \times 32 = 30 \times 16$

$\qquad = 60 \times 8$

$\qquad = 480$

Number

Lesson 4: **Dividing 2-digit numbers by single-digit numbers**

• Divide 2-digit numbers by single-digit numbers, with or without a remainder

Key words
• divide
• partitioning
• grouping

Discover

84 eggs are packaged in boxes that hold 6 eggs each. How many full boxes will there be?

You could think: How many groups of 6 make 84? If 10 groups of 6 make 60, that leaves 24 eggs. As 4 groups of 6 make 24, that makes 14 groups of 6 in all.

So, there will be 14 full boxes of eggs.

Learn

Using the partitioning strategy, you split the number to be divided into two parts: a multiple of the divisor, as large a multiple as possible, and a remaining number to be divided separately.

Add the results to find the answer.

Example

$91 \div 7 =$

91 = 70 (10 groups of 7) + 21 (3 groups of 7)

Add the groups of 7: $10 + 3 = 13$

56

Lesson 1: **Divisibility rules**

- Know and apply tests of divisibility by 2, 4, 5, 10, 25 and 100

Key words
- multiple
- divisibility rule
- factor
- common factor

Number

Discover

You can use special rules to test whether one whole number is divisible by another. Instead of dividing, you can use the rule to check if the number can be divided without a remainder.

Is 83 745 divisible by 5?

Is 38 414 divisible by 2?

Is 98 330 divisible by 10?

Learn and Example

A number is divisible by ...

Example

4 if the number formed by the last two digits is divisible by 4

7324 is divisible by 4 since 24 is divisible by 4

25 if the last two digits are 00, 25, 50 or 75

9275 is divisible by 25 since the last two digits are 75

100 if last two digits are 00

43 600 is divisibly by 100 since the last two digits are 00

Lesson 2: **Mental multiplication (1)**

Key words
• **multiply by**
• **compensation**
• **round**
• **adjust**
• **doubling**
• **halving**

- Use a range of mental strategies to multiply whole numbers

Discover

There are strategies to make multiplication easier. You can do some of them mentally or with jottings.

related facts

halving and doubling

compensation

Learn and Example

As with any other operation, when multiplying mentally you need to select the strategy that best suits the numbers you are working with.

Many of the strategies can be practised with smaller numbers and extended for use with larger numbers.

Strategy	Example
Related facts and place value	What is 40×700? I know 4×7 is 28, so 40×700 will be 28 000.
Compensation	What is 43×28? $43 \times 28 = 43 \times 30 - (43 \times 2)$ $ = 1290 - 86$ $ = 1204$
Halving and doubling	$16 \times 34 = 8 \times 68$ $ = 4 \times 136$ $ = 2 \times 272$ $ = 544$

Number

Lesson 3: **Doubling and halving**

Number

* Double or halve any 2-digit number

Discover

You can double numbers by partitioning them into parts for which you know the doubles. To double 33, you find the sum of double 30 and double 3, that is 66 (60 + 6). From this, you get a set of related doubles, for example: double 3·3 is 6·6, double 0·33 is 0·66.

Learn

You can use related number facts, with place value and partitioning, to find unknown doubles and halves.

Example

Double 64

64 = 60 + 4. Therefore: double 64 = double 60 + double 4 = 120 + 8 = 128

Double 6.4

Double 6·4 is 12·8 (ten times smaller than 128, the answer to double 64)

Half of 96

96 = 80 + 16. Therefore: half 96 = half 80 + half 16 = 40 + 8 = 48

Half of 9.6

Half 9·6 is 4·8 (ten times smaller than 48, the answer to half 96)

Lesson 4: **Making new number facts**

- Use known number facts to build new multiplication facts
- Explain and give examples of the rules of multiplication

Key words
- doubling
- halving
- multiplication fact
- factor
- rules of multiplication

Discover

You can use doubling to make new multiplication facts. If you know that 7×8 is 56 you also know that 14×8 is 112 and 28×8 is 224. Just double the answer for one to get the other!

8 times table				
$1 \times 8 = 8$	$2 \times 8 = 16$	$3 \times 8 = 24$	$4 \times 8 = 32$	$5 \times 8 = 40$
$6 \times 8 = 48$	$7 \times 8 = 56$	$8 \times 8 = 64$	$9 \times 8 = 72$	$10 \times 8 = 80$

Learn

You can make multiplication problems easier by breaking numbers into their factors.

Then you can rearrange the numbers in a preferred order.

You need to use two rules of multiplication:

- numbers can be multiplied in any order.
- three or more numbers can be grouped and multiplied in different ways.

Example
$$24 \times 17 = (4 \times 6) \times 17$$
$$= 4 \times (6 \times 17)$$
$$6 \times 17 = (6 \times 10) + (6 \times 7)$$
$$= 60 + 42$$
$$= 102$$
$$= 4 \times 102$$
$$= 408$$

Lesson 5: **Written multiplication (1)**

- Multiply 2-digit numbers by a single-digit number using a written method

Key words
- multiply
- estimate
- partition
- expanded method
- compact method (formal written method)

Number

Discover

Knowing written methods of calculation is very useful, particularly when mental multiplication is difficult. Both the grid and the expanded methods are good strategies.

You must understand place value before you can use them.

$76 \times 7 =$

×	70	6	
7	490	42	532

Learn

When you use the compact method to multiply you must be very careful where you write carried digits in case you confuse them with other digits. Write them in smaller figures, just above the answer line.

Example

$86 \times 6 =$

Grid method

×	80	6	
6	480	36	516

Expanded method

```
      8 6
  ×     6
  ─────────
      3 6    (6 × 6)
    4 8 0    (80 × 6)
  ─────────
    5 1 6
      1
```

Lesson 6: **Written multiplication (2)**

- Multiply 2-, 3- or 4-digit numbers by a single-digit number

Discover

If you buy multiple amounts of items in shops and supermarkets you often have to work with decimals.

If a DVD costs $19.38, what would 7 DVDs cost?

$19.38 × 7

Learn

You can use a written method, such as the expanded or formal method, to multiply $1938 by 7 then use place value to adjust the answer.

Example

1938 × 7 is 13 566. Therefore $19.38 × 7 is $135.66.

```
      1 9 3 8                  1 9 3 8
   ×         7              × 6 2 5 7
          5 6              1 3 5 6 6
        2 1 0
      6 3 0 0
      7 0 0 0
   1 3 5 6 6
```

Lesson 7: **Written division (1)**

- Divide 2- and 3-digit numbers by single-digit numbers, without remainders

Key words
- divide
- partitioning
- grouping

Number

Discover

You can use known facts and partitioning to divide a 3-digit number by a single-digit number.

Learn

Knowing how to divide a 3-digit number by a single-digit number is an important skill, particularly when dealing with money. You can use partitioning or grouping.

Example

$297 \div 9 =$

You know 9×3 is 27, so 9×30 is 270.

This means you can take a large 'chunk' from 297.

$297 - 270 = 27$.

$297 = 270 + 27$

So you can show the calculation in a simpler way:

$297 \div 9 = (270 \div 9) + (27 \div 9)$

$\qquad = 30 + 3$

$\qquad = 33$

The answer is 33.

Expanded written method

$$
\begin{array}{r}
3\ 3 \\
9\overline{\smash{)}\,2\ 9\ 7} \\
2\ 7\ 0 \quad (30 \times 9) \\
\hline
2\ 7 \\
-2\ 7 \quad (3 \times 9) \\
\hline
0
\end{array}
$$

63

Lesson 8: **Written division (2)**

- Divide 2- and 3-digit numbers by single-digit numbers, with or without a remainder

Key words
- divide
- partitioning
- grouping
- remainder
- formal method of division

Discover

When you divide one number by another, sometimes the division results in a perfect share with nothing left over.

364 beads divided equally between 4 people gives 91 beads each.

What happens if you divide the beads between 5 people? This gives 72 with 4 beads left over. The amount left over, after division, is the remainder.

You get remainders when the number you are dividing by is not a factor of the number being divided.

Learn

The formal method of division gives the answer more quickly as you record less information compared to other methods. Be careful when you use it – it is easier to make mistakes!

Example

$459 \div 8 =$

Expanded method	Compact method

Expanded method

```
      5 7 r 3
8)    4 5 9
   −  4 0 0   (50 × 8)
        5 9
   −    5 6   (7 × 8)
          3
```

Compact method

```
      5 7 r 3
8) 4 5 ⁵9
```

Lesson 1: **Mental multiplication (2)**

• Use place value and multiplication facts to multiply mentally

Key words
• multiplication fact
• place value

Number

Discover

Knowing one number fact helps you to find many others! If you know that 7 × 8 is 56, then you also know 70 × 8 is 560 and 700 × 8 is 5600.

$7 \times 8 = 56$

$70 \times 8 = 560$

$700 \times 8 = 5600$

Learn

When you are given a multiplication problem to solve, think:

Do I know a related multiplication fact that will help me solve this problem?

Example

To work out 900 × 4, think: Do I know a related fact? Yes!

9 × 4 is 36.
900 times 4 is 100 times 9 × 4, so the answer is 100 times 36. The answer is 3600.

To work out 0·9 × 4:

0·9 times 4 is 10 times smaller than 9 × 4, so the answer is 10 times smaller than 36. The answer is 3·6.

Lesson 2: **Long multiplication (1)**

* Use a written method to multiply 2-digit numbers by 2-digit numbers

Key words
* multiply
* estimate
* partition
* grid method
* expanded written method

Discover

You often need to multiply a 2-digit number by another 2-digit number.

Suppose 23 friends each had the same meal in a restaurant. If one meal cost $27, what was the total bill for the meal?

$27
23 people

Learn

To multiply together two 2-digit numbers, start with an estimate and then use a written strategy to solve the problem. Check the answer against the estimate.

> **Example**
>
> To work out 85×63, choose either the grid method or the expanded method.
>
> **Grid method**
>
> | × | 80 | 5 |
> |----|------|-----|
> | 60 | 4800 | 300 |
> | 3 | 240 | 15 |
>
> ```
>   5 1 0 0
> +   2 5 5
>   5 3 5 5
> ```
>
> **Expanded written method**
>
> ```
>       8 5
>   ×   6 3
> + 2 5¹5      (85 × 3)
>   5 1³0 0    (85 × 60)
>   5 3 5 5
> ```

66

Lesson 3: **Long multiplication (2)**

- Use a written method to multiply 2- or 3-digit numbers by 2-digit numbers

Key words
- multiply
- estimate
- partition
- formal written method

Number

Discover

Multiplying by large numbers can be difficult. Long multiplication is a special method for multiplying two large numbers. It works by splitting the multiplication into manageable parts.

$$
\begin{array}{r}
4\ 3\ 2 \\
\times\quad\quad 5\ 4 \\
\hline
1\ 7\ {}^12\ 8 \\
2\ 1\ {}^16\ {}^10\ 0 \\
\hline
8 \\
\hline
\end{array}
$$

Learn

When you use the compact form of long multiplication you have to be very careful where you write carried digits. Write them as small numbers just to the right of the next place value column so that you don't confuse them with other digits.

Example

$285 \times 63 =$

Expanded method

$$
\begin{array}{r}
2\ 8\ 5 \\
\times\quad 6\ 3 \\
\hline
8\ {}^25\ {}^15 \\
1\ 7\ {}^51\ {}^30\ 0 \\
\hline
1\ 7\ 9\ 5\ 5 \\
\hline
\end{array}
$$

(285×3)
(285×60)

Compact method

$$
\begin{array}{r}
2\ 8\ 5 \\
\times\quad 6\ 3 \\
\hline
8\ {}^25\ {}^15 \\
1\ 7\ {}^51\ {}^30\ 0 \\
\hline
1\ 7\ 9\ 5\ 5 \\
\hline
\end{array}
$$

The answer is 17955.

Lesson 4: **Mental division**

- Use place value and division facts to divide mentally

Key words
- divide
- partitioning
- grouping

Discover

It is useful to be able to divide mentally when dealing with money and measurements. Leon has $9.20 to share equally between himself and his three friends. His friend suggests that he finds a related fact and adjusts it by place value. What fact would this be?

$9.20

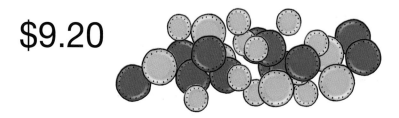

Learn

You can use closely related facts to divide a decimal by a whole number.

Example

$4{\cdot}2 \div 7 =$

As you know that $42 \div 7 = 6$, you also know $4{\cdot}2 \div 7 = 0{\cdot}6$.

($4{\cdot}2$ is 10 times smaller than 42, so the answer will be 10 times smaller than 6.)

$4{\cdot}2 \div 7 = 0{\cdot}6$

Lesson 5: **Division with remainders**

- Divide three-digit numbers by single-digit numbers
- Express remainders as numbers, fractions and decimals

Key words
- divisible by
- remainder
- whole number
- fraction
- decimal

Number

Discover

$$\overset{104 \text{ r.1}}{4\overline{)4\,1\,17}}$$

What should be done with the remainder?

Learn

Dividing numbers doesn't always end with a whole number as the answer. Often there is a remainder.

We can deal with the remainder in different ways.

It can be written as a number:

$417 \div 4 = 104$ r.1.

It also can be written as a fraction, because the 1 left over can be split into 4 to make a fraction:

$417 \div 4 = 104\frac{1}{4}$.

This answer can also be written as a decimal because $\frac{1}{4}$ is the same as 0.25.

$417 \div 4 = 104.25$

Example

What is $626 \div 5$?

Express the remainder as a number, a fraction and a decimal.

$$\overset{125 \text{ r.1}}{5\overline{)6^12^26}}$$

$626 \div 5 = 125$ remainder 1

The remainder 1 can be divided by 5 and written as a fraction.

$626 \div 5 = 125\frac{1}{5}$

The fraction can be written as a decimal because $\frac{1}{5}$ is equal to 0.2

$626 \div 5 = 125.2$

Lesson 6: **Long division**

- Use the expanded written method of long division to divide 3- or 4-digit numbers by 2-digit numbers

Key words
- divisible by
- estimate
- partition

Discover

You often need to divide a 3- or 4-digit number by a 2-digit number. Suppose 24 construction workers must build equal sections of a brick wall. If the wall is 648 m long, what share of the wall will each worker build?

648 m
24 workers

Learn

The expanded written method for solving division problems is based on repeated subtraction of 'chunks' – the largest possible tens and units multiples of the divisor.

Example

To work out 896 ÷ 28, the expanded written method looks like this.

```
          3 2
   28 ) 8 9 6
       − 8 4 0    (30 × 28)
           5 6
       −   5 6    (2 × 28)
             0
```

The answer is 32.

Lesson 7: **Fractions of quantities (1)**

- Use a fraction as an operator to find the fraction of a quantity

Key words
- numerator
- denominator
- unit fraction
- non-unit fraction

Number

Discover

As well as being numbers, fractions are also operators. They can 'operate' on a quantity to change its value. For proper fractions, the outcome would be smaller than the original quantity.

In shops, you see signs advertising price reductions such as: '$\frac{1}{2}$ off original price', '$\frac{2}{3}$ off marked price'.

Learn

To find a non-unit fraction of a quantity:

1 Find one part (unit fraction) by dividing the quantity by the denominator.
2 Find the required number of parts by multiplying the unit fraction by the numerator.

Example

$\frac{9}{10}$ of $80 =

- divide the whole quantity into 10 parts (unit fraction):
  $80 ÷ 10 = $8
- multiply the unit fraction by 9: $8 × 9 = $72

Number

Lesson 8: **Fractions of quantities (2)**

- Use a fraction as an operator to find the fraction of a quantity

Key words
- numerator
- denominator
- unit fraction
- non-unit fraction

Discover

You often find percentage forms of fractions in news reports.

A survey might say: '31% of teenagers want a smartphone' or '79% of people pay no attention to adverts on TV'.

In other words, $\frac{31}{100}$ of teenagers want a smartphone and $\frac{79}{100}$ of people don't pay attention to TV advertising.

43%
of young people have walked into something or someone while checking their phone

Learn

To find a non-unit fraction of a quantity:

1 Find one part (unit fraction) by dividing the quantity by the denominator.

2 Find the required number of parts by multiplying the unit fraction by the numerator.

Example

$\frac{31}{100}$ of 2700 km =

- divide the whole quantity into 100 parts (unit fraction): 2700 ÷ 100 = 27
- work out 31 parts by multiplying the unit fraction by 31: 31 × 27 = 837 km.

Lesson 1: **Polygons (1)**

• Classify different polygons and understand whether a 2D shape is a polygon or not

Key words
• regular polygon
• irregular polygon
• angle

Discover

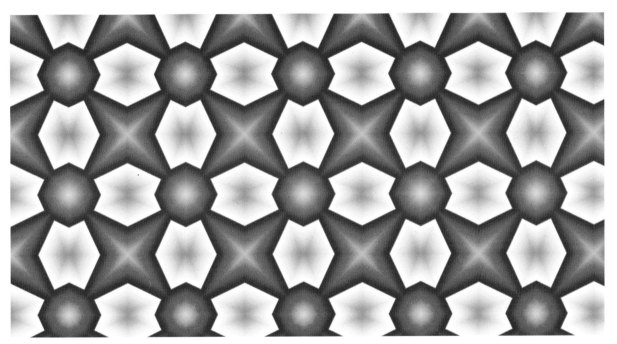

Learn

Polygons can be **regular** – all angles are equal and all sides are equal, or **irregular** – the angles may be of different measures and the sides may be different lengths.

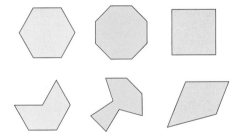

Example

Which shapes are NOT polygons? Which shape is irregular?

Shapes B, D and F are not polygons. D and F are not enclosed and B has curved segments.

Shape E is an irregular triangle, as its sides are different lengths and its angles are different sizes.

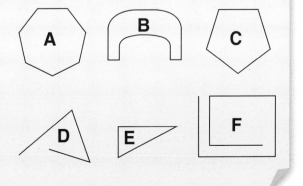

Lesson 2: **Polygons (2)**

- Classify different polygons and decide whether a polygon is convex or concave

Key words
- diagonal
- vertices
- concave
- convex
- acute
- obtuse

Discover

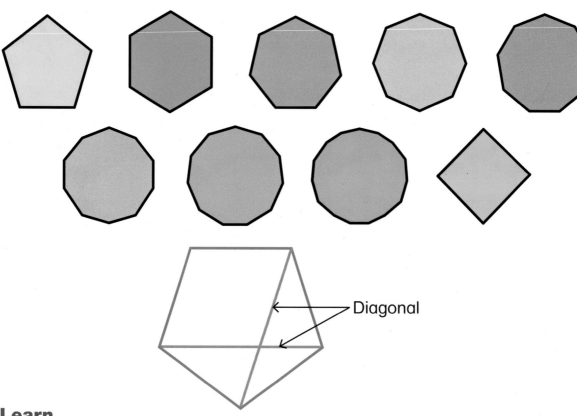

Diagonal

Learn

A polygon is convex if it has no 'dents' (indentations) in it. Otherwise, the shape is concave.

Example

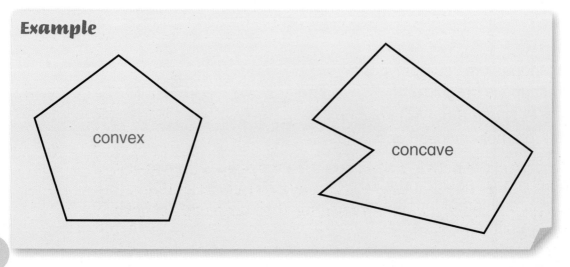

convex

concave

74

Lesson 3: **Quadrilaterals (1)**

- Identify and describe properties of quadrilaterals and classify using parallel sides, equal sides, equal angles

Key words
- parallel
- perpendicular
- quadrilateral
- parallelogram
- rhombus
- trapezium
- kite

Discover

Geometry

Learn

A quadrilateral is a polygon that has four sides – and four vertices and four angles.

Quadrilaterals can be classified by whether or not their sides, angles, diagonals or vertices have particular properties.

Example

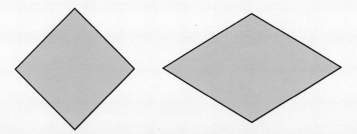

The shape on the right is a rhombus. Like the square (turned 45°), it has four sides of equal length, its opposite sides are parallel and its angles are equal. Unlike squares, rhombuses do not have right angles.

Lesson 4: **Quadrilaterals (2)**

- Identify and describe properties of quadrilaterals and classify using parallel sides, equal sides, equal angles

Discover

Key words
- parallel
- perpendicular
- adjacent
- quadrilateral
- trapezium
- parallelogram
- rhombus
- kite

Geometry

Learn

A rhombus is a parallelogram with four equal sides. Unlike a square, a rhombus has opposite and equal acute angles, and opposite and equal obtuse angles. A line joining two points on dotted paper can form a side of several different rhombuses.

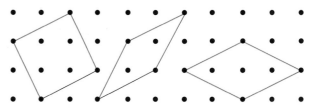

Example

Could you include a trapezium in this Venn diagram?

No, a trapezium has only one pair of parallel sides. All parallelograms have two pairs of parallel sides.

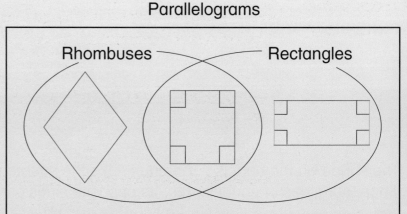

Lesson 1: **Visualising 3D shapes**

Key words
• prism
• pyramid
• cube
• edge
• face
• vertex

• Visualise and describe the properties of 3D shapes,
e.g. faces, edges and vertices

Discover

Geometry

Learn

A shape is still the same shape, whatever its position or size.
This pyramid is still a pyramid, no matter what position it is in.

A cross-section is what you see
when you slice through something.

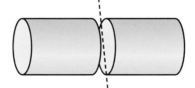

Example

These are the cross-sections of some prisms.

A – pentagonal prism

B – hexagonal prism

C – triangular prism

D – cube or cuboid

77

Lesson 2: **Constructing 3D shapes**

Key words
• prism
• pyramid
• cuboid
• tetrahedron
• octahedron

• Recognise, describe and build simple 3D shapes

Discover

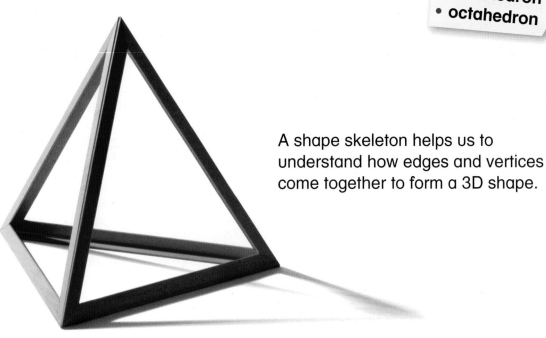

A shape skeleton helps us to understand how edges and vertices come together to form a 3D shape.

Learn

To construct the skeleton of a 3D shape think about the shape of the faces and how they meet at the edges.

Example

A hexagonal-based prism consists of two hexagons, which form the bases and six rectangles, which form the faces that connect the bases.

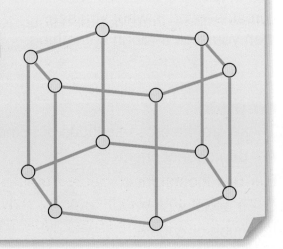

Geometry

Lesson 3: **Nets (1)**

- Use knowledge of the properties of cubes to identify and draw different nets of cubes

Key words
- cube
- square
- net
- base
- side
- vertex

Discover

A net is what a 3D shape would look like if it was opened out flat.

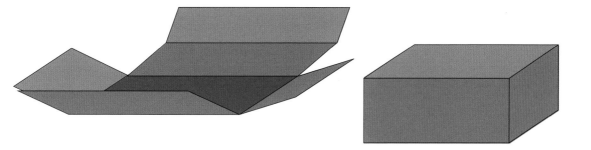

Geometry

Learn

There may be several nets for one shape, like these for a closed cube.

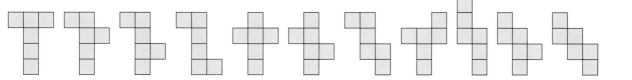

Example

Which is the correct net for a square-based pyramid?

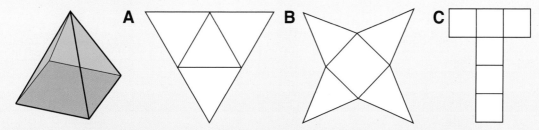

Net **B** is the net for a square-based pyramid. It is the only one of these three nets with the correct polygonal shapes to construct a square-based pyramid: a square and four triangles.

Lesson 4: **Nets (2)**

- Use knowledge of prisms and pyramids to identify and draw nets of these shapes

Key words
- prism
- pyramid
- net
- base
- side
- vertex

Discover

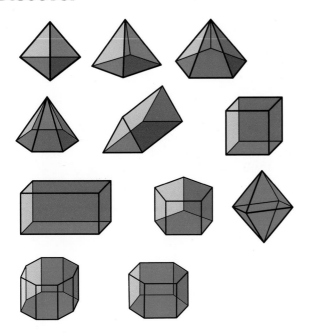

Geometry

Learn

The net of a shape can identify:

- its base(s): the number of triangular faces extending from one base (a pyramid)

- the number of parallelograms connecting two bases (a prism).

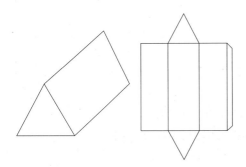

Example

Which of these nets will form prisms?

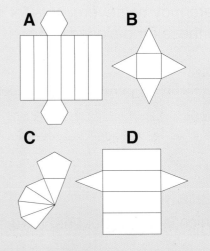

Nets A and D will both form prisms – they have two identical polygonal bases and side faces that are parallelograms.

Nets B and C will form pyramids – they have multiple, identical triangles forming side faces; the remaining face is the base.

Lesson 1: **Measuring angles**

• Estimate angles to the nearest degree and
  measure them using a protractor

Discover

Benchmark angles

45°   90°   180°

Learn

Use what you know about the size of some angles to make
an estimate of an unknown angle.

Benchmark angles, such as 45°, 90° and 180°, can be used
to compare and estimate an approximate measurement.

> ### Example
> Estimate the size of the angle.
>
>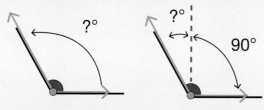
>
> ?°   ?°   90°
>
> Split the angle in two parts: 90° plus an unknown angle.
> Then use benchmark angles to estimate the remaining angle:
> less than 45°, about 35°.
> The angle is estimated to be 125°.

Geometry

Lesson 2: **Drawing angles**

Key words
- angle
- protractor

- Draw acute and obtuse angles and use a protractor to measure to the nearest degree

Discover

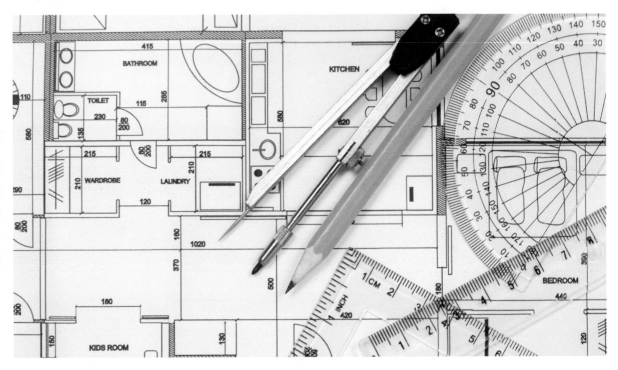

Learn

When drawing angles, mark a point on the line to show the position of the vertex – this is where to centre the protractor.

Example

Draw an angle of 143°.

- Draw a straight line – an arm of the angle.
- Mark a dot on the line – the vertex.
- Centre the protractor over the dot and the baseline along the arm of the angle.
- Mark a dot at 143° on the scale.
- Remove the protractor.
- Join the dot to the vertex with a ruler.

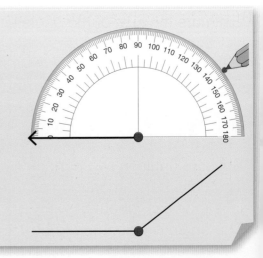

Lesson 3: **Angles in a triangle**

- Calculate angles in a triangle

Discover

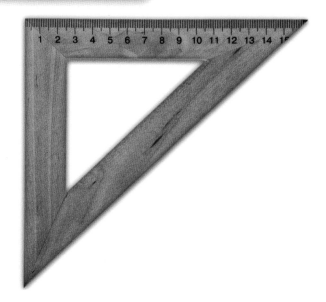

Learn

How many degrees are in a triangle?

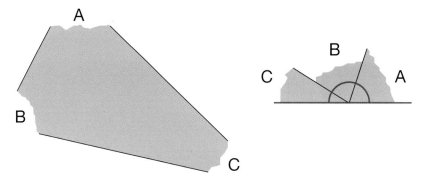

Rule: The sum of the interior angles of any triangle equals 180°.

Example

Find the missing angle, A.

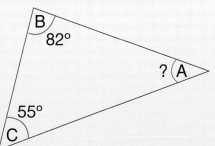

$A + B + C = 180°$

$A = 180° - (B + C)$

$\quad = 180° - (82° + 55°)$

$\quad = 180° - 137°$

$\quad = 43°$

Angle A is 43°.

Geometry

83

Lesson 4: **Angles around a point**

- Calculate angles around a point

Geometry

Discover

There are 360 degrees in a circle.

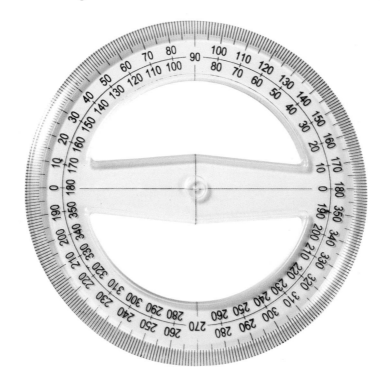

Learn

Rule: The sum of angles around a point will always be 360 degrees.

Example

What is the missing angle, A?

$A + B + C + D + E = 360°$

$A = 360° − (B + C + D + E)$

$\quad = 360° − (114° + 77° + 51° + 62°)$

$\quad = 360° − 304°$

$\quad = 56°$

Angle A is 56°.

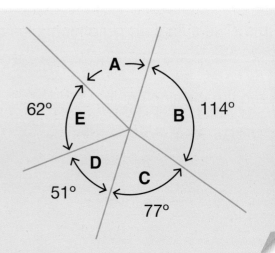

Lesson 1: **Plotting co-ordinates (1)**

Key words
- co-ordinates
- quadrant
- *x*-axis
- *y*-axis
- *x*-co-ordinate
- *y*-co-ordinate

- Read and plot co-ordinates in all four quadrants

Discover

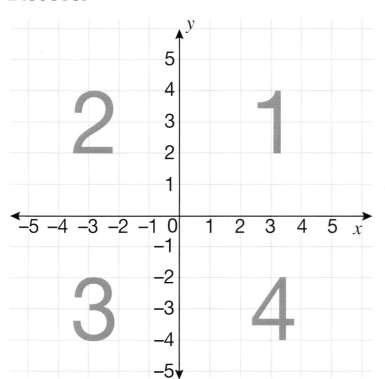

Geometry

Learn

To plot points in all four quadrants:

<u>*x*-co-ordinate:</u> From the origin, move horizontally along the *x*-axis. If the *x*-co-ordinate is positive, move right; if the *x*-co-ordinate is negative, move left.

<u>*y*-co-ordinate:</u> From the *x*-co-ordinate, move vertically along the *y*-axis. If the *y*-co-ordinate is positive, move up; if the *y*-co-ordinate is negative, move down.

Draw a point at the location.

Example

Plot $(-3, -2)$.

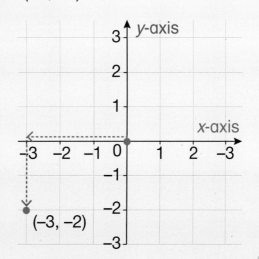

$(-3, -2)$

85

Lesson 2: **Plotting co-ordinates (2)**

• Read and plot co-ordinates in all four quadrants

Discover

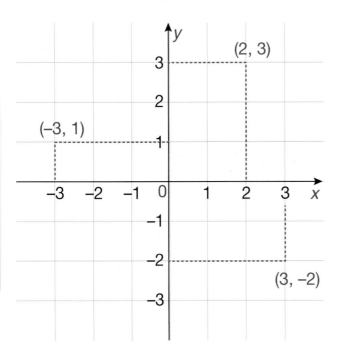

Geometry

Learn

Properties of 2D shapes can help locate the missing vertex of a shape on a co-ordinate plane.

Example

The co-ordinates for three vertices of a rectangle are A (1, 1), B (5, 1), C (5, 6).

The missing vertex D will have the same *x*-co-ordinate as vertex A (1) and the same *y*-co-ordinate as vertex C (6).

So, vertex D has the co-ordinates (1, 6).

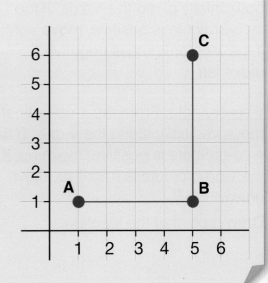

Lesson 3: **Reflection (1)**

- Predict where a polygon will be after one reflection

Discover

Geometry

Learn

To reflect a shape, reflect the vertices and join them to form the image.

1 Measure the perpendicular distance from the vertex to the mirror line.

2 Measure the same perpendicular distance on the other side and plot the image.

3 Connect the plots to reflect the original object.

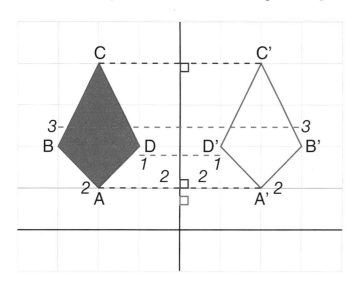

Lesson 4: **Reflection (2)**

- Predict where a polygon will be after one reflection, where the sides of the shape are not parallel or perpendicular to the mirror line

Key words
- **image**
- **reflect**
- **quadrant**
- **negative**
- **x-axis**
- **y-axis**

Discover

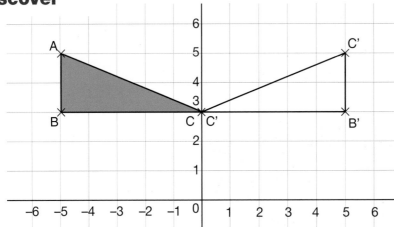

Learn

You can reflect a simple shape across both axes *x* and *y*.

First, reflect the vertices in one axis. Then, reflect the vertices of the image in the second axis to give a second image.

Example

The co-ordinates of a triangle are (2, 2), (4, 1), (4, 6). What are the co-ordinates following reflection in the *y*-axis, then the *x*-axis?

Use perpendicular distance to determine the new image co-ordinates:
(−2, −2), (−4, −1), (−4, −6).

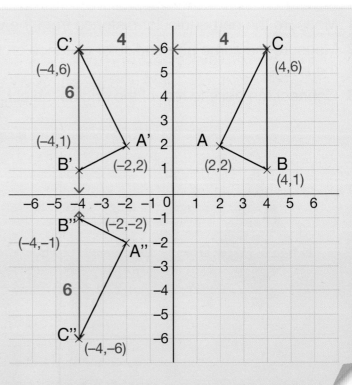

Lesson 5: **Translation (1)**

• Identify the position of a shape after a translation in the first quadrant of a co-ordinate grid and know that the shape has not changed

Geometry

Discover

A translation is when a shape is moved from one location to another without changing its size, shape or orientation.

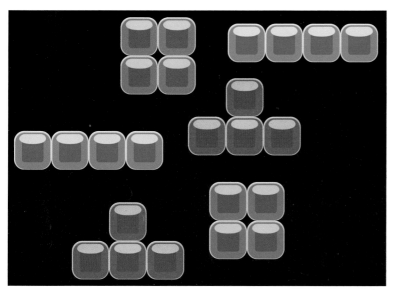

Learn

You can translate an object to the left, right, down, up, or any combination of directions. In translation, every vertex of a shape moves in the same direction, by the same amount.

Example

Triangle ABC is translated 3 squares up, 2 squares right.

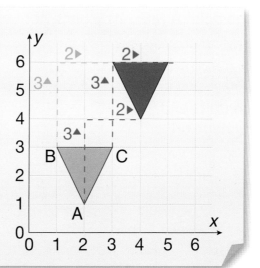

Lesson 6: **Translation (2)**

- Translate shapes into all four quadrants using co-ordinates

Geometry

Discover

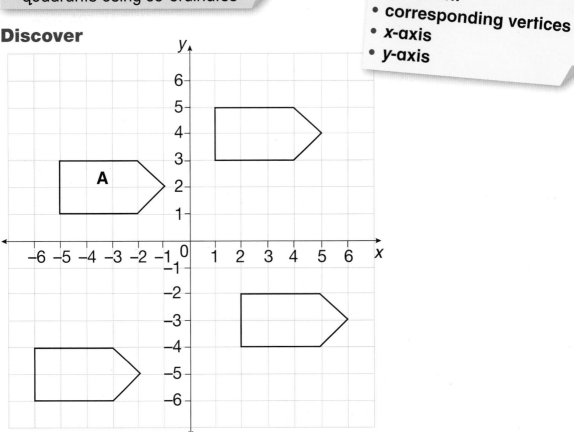

Learn

We can determine the new positions of co-ordinates after translation with or without using a co-ordinates grid.

Translate the point A (−3, −4) 5 units right and 7 units up.

Example

With a grid

Take each point and move it as directed.

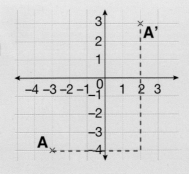

Without a grid

Add the translation to the original co-ordinate.

Original (−3, −4) + translation (+5, +7)

−3 + 5 = 2, −4 + 7 = 3

So the new co-ordinate will be (2, 3)

Lesson 7: **Rotation (1)**

• Identify, describe and represent the position
  of a shape following a rotation of 90°

Discover

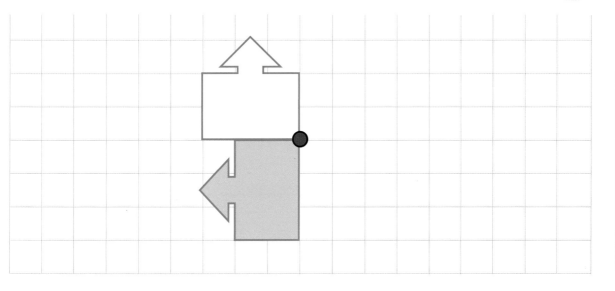

Learn

An object and its image after rotation are the same shape
and size, but they may be facing different directions.

Example

An easy way to rotate
a shape is to trace it
on tracing paper, then
rotate the tracing paper
about the centre of
rotation, as shown.

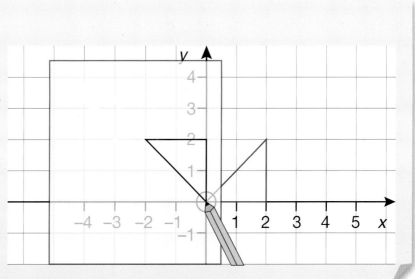

Geometry

Lesson 8: **Rotation (2)**

- Rotate a shape about one of its vertices in all four quadrants using co-ordinates

Key words
- rotate
- quadrant
- negative
- corresponding vertices
- *x*-axis
- *y*-axis

Discover

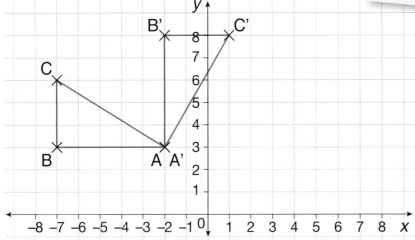

Geometry

Learn

To rotate a shape 90° around one vertex, rotate one side, then locate the other vertices relative to this side.

Here, side AD has been rotated 90° clockwise about vertex A. The positions of B' and C' have been found using the distances of B and C from vertices A and D.

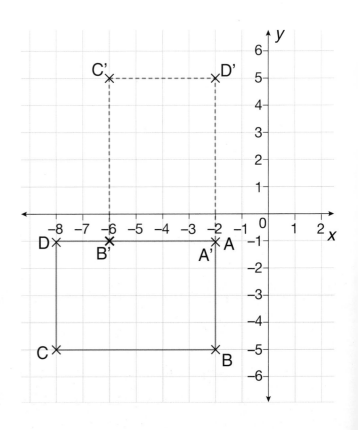

Lesson 1: **Converting units**

- Convert between units of length (km, m, cm and mm) using decimals to 3 places

Discover

Knowing the relationship between different units of length will help with conversion.

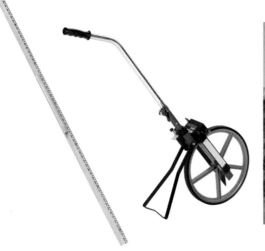

NEXT 3 km

400 m

Learn

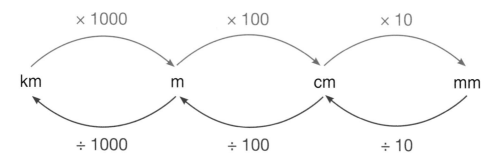

× 1000   × 100   × 10

km   m   cm   mm

÷ 1000   ÷ 100   ÷ 10

Example

$4.827 \text{ m} + 344.5 \text{ cm} =$

Step 1: Convert 344.5 cm to metres $= 3.445$ m

Step 2: Complete the addition

$4.827 \text{ m} + 3.445 \text{ m} = 8.272 \text{ m}$

To convert back to mixed units

$8.272 \text{ m} = 8 \text{ m} + (0.272 \text{ m} \times 100) = 8 \text{ m } 27.2 \text{ cm}$

Measure

Lesson 2: **Problems involving length**

- Use all four operations and decimals to solve problems involving length

Key words
- unit
- kilometre (km)
- metre (m)
- centimetre (cm)
- millimetre (mm)
- decimal place

Discover

To solve problems involving length, it is often necessary to convert between units.

Learn

To solve a word problem:

- Step 1: Identify the exact question to answer.
- Step 2: Find clue words that identify the operation to use.

Example

A fence is to be built around a garden.
The garden measures 7 m 56·5 cm by 9 m.
How many 2·5 m fence panels will be needed?

Step 1: You need to work out the perimeter of the garden in metres and then divide by 2·5 m to work out how many fence panels you will need.

Step 2: You know perimeter of a regular rectangle = length + width × 2
= 7 m 56·5 cm + 9 m × 2
= 7·565 m + 9 m × 2
= 33·13 m.
33·13 m ÷ 2·5 m = 13·252
So, you will need 14 fence panels.

Measure

Lesson 3: **Drawing and measuring lines**

Key words
• centimetre (cm)
• millimetre (mm)

• Draw and measure lines to the nearest centimetre and millimetre

Discover

Measure

Learn

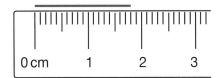

We can use a ruler to measure to the nearest millimetre, then round to the nearest centimetre.

It important to line up the zero mark of the ruler with the end of the object being measured.

Be careful: some rulers have the zero mark at the starting edge and some have an indented zero mark.

Example
Write the length of the line to the nearest:
a millimetre, **b** centimetre.

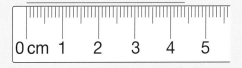

a To the nearest millimetre, the length of the line is 44 mm (4 cm 4 mm).

b To the nearest centimetre, the length of the line is 4 cm.

95

Lesson 4: Imperial units

Key words
* metric
* imperial
* approximately equal to (≈)
* estimate
* mile

• Convert and make approximate conversions between miles and kilometres

Discover

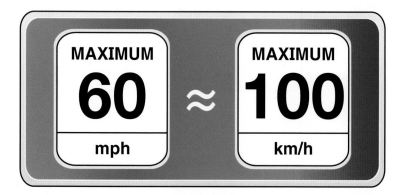

1 mile ≈ 1.6 km
(or 1600m)

Learn

The imperial system uses miles rather than kilometres for length. Some countries measure road distances in miles and some use kilometres.

1 kilometre is approximately $\frac{5}{8}$ miles: 1 km ≈ $\frac{5}{8}$ miles

8 kilometres is approximately 5 miles: 8 km ≈ 5 miles

1 mile is approximately $\frac{8}{5}$ km: 1 mile ≈ $\frac{8}{5}$ km

5 miles is approximately 8 km: 5 miles ≈ 8 km

Example

Mr Jones is on holiday. While driving, he sees the following sign:

> LONDON   115 miles

Approximately how many kilometres is Mr Jones from London?

5 miles ≈ 8 km

(115 ÷ 5) × 8 = 23 × 8

                = 184

So 115 miles ≈ 184 km

Measure

96

Lesson 1: **Converting units**

- Convert between units of mass (kg, g), using decimals to 3 places

Discover

It is easier to work with measurements that are in the same unit rather than mixed units.

Learn

1 kg = 1000 g

To convert kilograms to grams, multiply by 1000.

Example

Baby Tara weighs 3 kg 84 g. Baby Mia weighs 4795 g. Baby Rose weighs 4 kg 7 g

What is their combined weight in kg?

$$3 \text{ kg } 84 \text{ g} = 3084 \text{ g}$$
$$4 \text{ kg } 7 \text{ g} = 4007 \text{ g}$$
$$3084 \text{ g} + 4795 \text{ g} + 4007 \text{ g} = 11\,098 \text{ g}$$
$$= 11 \text{ kg } 98 \text{ g}$$

Measure

Lesson 2: **Problems involving mass**

• Use all four operations and decimals to solve problems involving mass

Discover

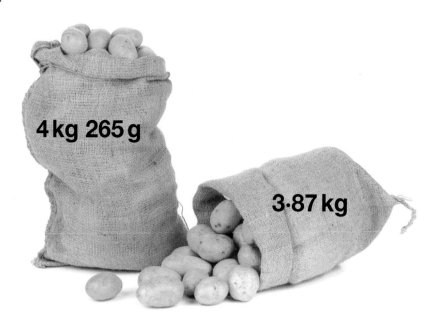

4 kg 265 g

3·87 kg

Measure

Learn

To solve problems involving mass, you may need to convert between units.

The potatoes are labelled 4 kg 265 g and 3·87 kg. To find the difference in mass, convert both masses to grams: 4265 g and 3870 g.

To make it easier to convert a decimal number of kilograms into grams, annex zeros to the number before converting. Writing zeroes after a decimal does not change the value of the number.

Example

Boxes A and B weigh 3·895 kg and 4·4 kg. What is the combined mass of the boxes?

3·895 kg

4·4 kg

Total mass = 3·895 kg + 4·4 kg
= 3·895 kg + 4·400 kg
= 3895 g + 4400 g
= 8295 g or 8·295 kg

Lesson 3: **Different scales**

- Interpret and compare readings on different scales, including between divisions

📌 **Key words**
- mass
- kilogram (kg)
- gram (g)
- scale
- division

Discover

Which of these readings can be read more accurately?

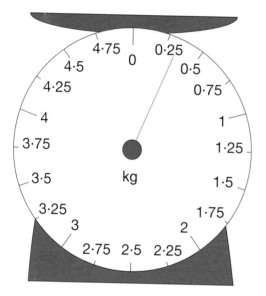 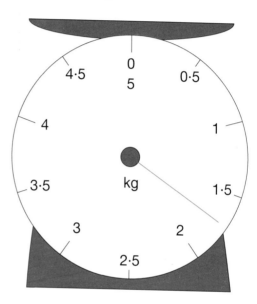

Learn

You can read scales accurately if you know the value of each scale division.
To read a scale between intervals:

- Identify two labelled divisions, such as 100 g and 200 g.
- Count the number of intervals or 'jumps' between these amounts.
- Use the division to work out the value of one interval.
- Count along the scale to check the interval is correct.

Example

There are 5 equal divisions between each 100 g, each division is equal to 20 g. The reading is halfway between 240 g and 260 g: 250 g

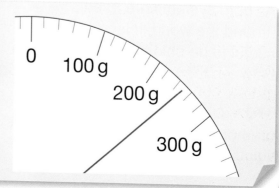

Measure

Lesson 4: **Imperial units**

- Convert and make approximate conversions between pounds and kilograms

Discover

Mountain Pride Tomatoes

$ 2.00 lb

Measure

Learn

For mass, the imperial system uses stones, pounds and ounces, rather than grams and kilograms.

As both systems are used around the world, it is useful to be able to convert between them.

1 kg ≈ 2 lb
or, more accurately:
1 kg ≈ 2·2 lb

Example

Approximately how many kilograms of carrots can you buy for $5?

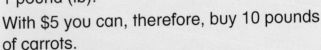

CARROTS
$0.50 per 1 lb

Carrots are $0.50 for 1 pound (lb).

With $5 you can, therefore, buy 10 pounds of carrots.

Convert 10 lb to kilograms:

Using 1 kg ≈ 2 lb: (10 ÷ 2) × 1 kg = 5 kg

Using 1 kg ≈ 2·2 lb: (10 ÷ 2·2) × 1 kg = 4·55 kg

Lesson 1: **Converting units**

- Convert between units of capacity (*l*, ml), using decimals to 3 places

Key words
- litre (*l*)
- millilitre (ml)

Discover

3700 ml   2·9 *l*

It is easier to work with measurements that are in the same unit rather than in mixed units.

1 *l* = 1000 ml

Learn

To convert litres to millilitres, multiply by 1000.

Example

Two jugs have a combined capacity of 7·6 litres. If Jug A has a capacity of 4 *l* 875 ml, what is the capacity of Jug B?

7·6 *l* = 4 *l* 875 ml + Jug B

Jug B = 7·6 *l* − 4 *l* 875 ml (rearranging the number sentence)

    = 7600 − 4875 ml

    = 2725 ml (or 2·725 *l*)

Jug B has a capacity of 2·725 *l*.

Measure

101

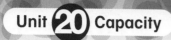
Lesson 2: **Problems involving capacity**

Key words
• litre (*l*)
• millilitre (ml)

• Use all four operations and decimals to solve problems involving capacity

Discover

2*l* 455 ml

6·25*l*

In order to solve problems that involve capacity, it is often necessary to convert between litres and millilitres.

Learn

It is easier to convert a decimal number of litres into millilitres if you annex zeros to the number before converting. Remember, writing zeros after a decimal does not change the value of the number.

Example

Buckets A and B have capacities 5*l* 262 ml and 3·8*l*.
What is the total capacity of the buckets?

5*l* 262 ml + 3·8*l* = 5·262*l* + 3·800*l*
            = 9·062*l*

or

5*l* 262 ml + 3·8*l* = 5262 ml + 3800 ml
            = 9062 ml
            = 9·062*l*

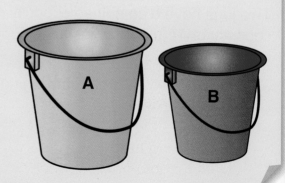

Measure

Lesson 3: **Different scales**

- Interpret and compare readings on different scales, including between divisions

Key words
- litre (*l*)
- millilitre (ml)

Discover

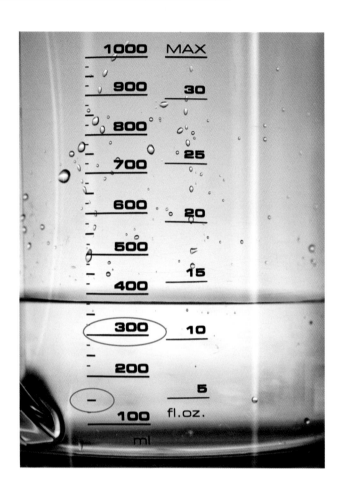

Measure

Learn

To read a scale between intervals:

- Identify two labelled divisions, such as 100 ml and 200 ml.
- Count the number of intervals, or 'jumps' between these amounts.
- Use the division to work out the value of one interval.
- Count along the scale to check the interval is correct.

Example

There are 3 divisions between each numbered interval. They each mark 25 ml.

There is 125 ml of liquid in this container.

100 ml

103

Lesson 4: **Imperial units**

- Convert and make approximate conversions between pints and litres

Key words
- metric
- imperial
- litre (*l*)
- approximately equal to (≈)
- estimate
- pint
- symbol

Discover

Learn

The imperial system is an older system of measurements. It uses pints, gallons and quarts, rather than litres and millilitres, for capacity.

As both metric and imperial units are used in different countries across the world, it is useful to be able to convert between the two systems.

$1\,l \approx 1{\cdot}75$ pints

Example

John is from the UK and visits the United States. He buys 5 litres of milk. How many pints is that?

Convert 5 pints to litres.

$1\,l \approx 1.75$ pints

5 litres $\approx 5 \times 1.75 = 8.75$

John buys 8.75 pints of milk.

Lesson 1: **Telling and comparing the time**

- Tell the time using digital and analogue clocks using the 24-hour clock
- Compare times on digital and analogue clocks

Discover

We can compare times on digital and analogue clocks by converting between the two formats.

24-hour time

| 0 | 1 | 2 | 3 | 4 | 5 | 6 | 7 | 8 | 9 | 10 | 11 | 12 | 13 | 14 | 15 | 16 | 17 | 18 | 19 | 20 | 21 | 22 | 23 |

a.m.   **p.m.**

| 12 | 1 | 2 | 3 | 4 | 5 | 6 | 7 | 8 | 9 | 10 | 11 | 12 | 1 | 2 | 3 | 4 | 5 | 6 | 7 | 8 | 9 | 10 | 11 |

12-hour time

Learn

To convert from 12-hour to 24-hour clock:

- between 12:00 a.m. and 12:59 a.m., subtract 12 hours: 12:37 a.m. is 00:37

- between 1:00 a.m. and 12:59 p.m., no change, but hours below 10, insert a 0 in front: 7:00 a.m. is 07:00

- between 1:00 p.m. and 11:59 p.m., add 12 hours: 10:57 p.m. is 22:57.

Example

Which is later: 10:50 p.m. or 22:45?

Convert to 24-hour clock times.

10:50 p.m. is 22:50
((10 + 12):50)

22:50 is later than 22:45.

Therefore, 10:50 p.m. is the later time.

Measure

105

Lesson 2: **Converting units of time**

> **Key words**
> * day
> * week
> * month
> * year
> * decade
> * century

• Recognise and convert one unit of time into another

Discover

Time is not metric, so we need to be careful when converting from one unit to another.

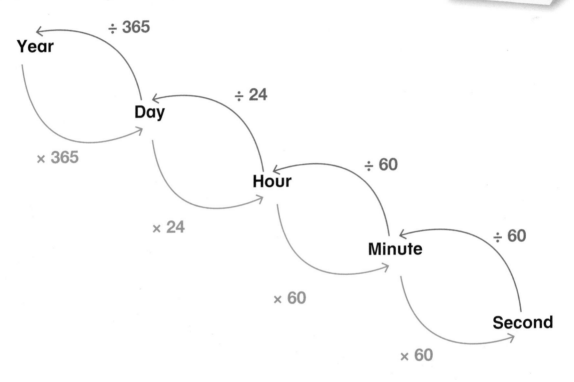

Year   ÷ 365

× 365

Day   ÷ 24

× 24

Hour   ÷ 60

× 60

Minute   ÷ 60

× 60

Second

Learn

60 seconds is 1 minute.

60 minutes is 1 hour.

24 hours is 1 day.

7 days is 1 week.

365 days, 52 weeks or 12 months is 1 year.

10 years is 1 decade.

100 years is 1 century.

Example

What is 40 days in weeks and days?

7 days is 1 week, so 40 days is:

$40 \div 7 = 5$ r 5 or 5 weeks and 5 days

Lesson 3: **Time intervals**

- Calculate time intervals using digital and analogue times, and in days, months and years

Discover

5 hours

September

Su	Mo	Tu	We	Th	Fr	Sa
						①
2	3	4	5	6	7	8
9	10	11	12	13	14	15
16	17	18	19	20	21	22
23	24	25	26	27	28	29
30	31					

Learn

The length of time from the starting time to an ending time is called 'elapsed time'. When calculating elapsed time, we add the units of time separately.

Example

Daisy leaves home to go to school at 07:41 and returns at 16:27. How long was she away?

Split the problem into smaller intervals by bridging to the nearest hour, 12 noon or multiples of hours:

19 min   4 hours   4 hours   27 min

07:41 08:00   12:00   16:00 16:27

The total time Daisy spent away from home
= 19 min + 4 h + 4 h + 27 min = 8 h 46 min

Measure

Lesson 4: **Time zones**

- Appreciate how the time is different around the world

Key words
- time zones
- degrees of longitude

Discover

It would not make sense for the whole planet to be on the same time, so the world has to be divided into different time zones.

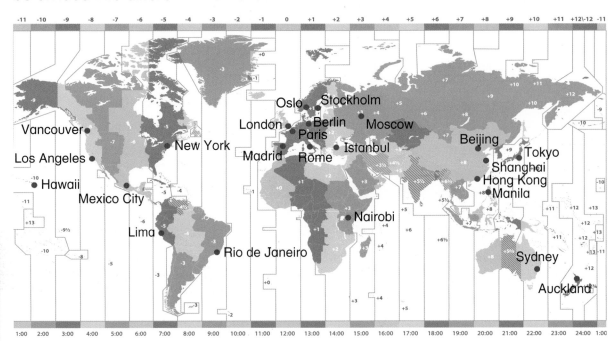

Learn

The world is divided into 24 time zones. Clocks are set one hour apart in adjacent time zones.

Example

Jun lives in New York. His uncle lives in Beijing. If it is 10 a.m. in New York what time is it in Beijing?

The time zone for New York is –5 and the time zone for Beijing is +8. Therefore, New York and Beijing are 13 (5 + 8) time zones apart.

The time in Beijing is 11 p.m. (10 a.m. + 13 hours)

Measure

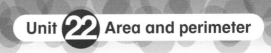
Lesson 1: **Perimeter (1)**

• Calculate the perimeter of rectangles

📌 **Key words**
• **length**
• **width**
• **perimeter**
• **centimetre (cm)**
• **metre (m)**

Discover

The perimeter of a rectangle = length + width × 2

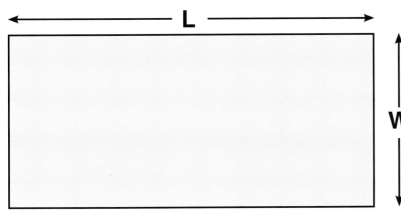

$P = 2(L + W)$

Learn

The perimeter of a rectangle can be found using one of three methods:

• Measure and find the sum of the sides.

• Find the sum of double the length and double the width. The rule is $P = 2(L + W)$.

• For a square, where all four sides are equal, multiply the length of one side by 4.

Perimeter

$$2L \ + \ 2W \ = \ P$$

length   width perimeter

Example

What is the perimeter of a garden lawn if the length is 8 m and the width is 3 m?

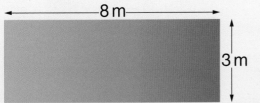

P = ?

$P = 2(L + W)$
$= 2(8\,m + 3\,m)$
$= 2 \times 11\,m$
$= 22\,m$

Measure

Lesson 2: **Perimeter (2)**

• Calculate the perimeter of rectilinear shapes

Discover

Measure

Learn

'Cutting the corner' out of a rectangle preserves its perimeter. Rather than adding together all the individual side lengths, you can find the perimeter by thinking of it as a single rectangle.

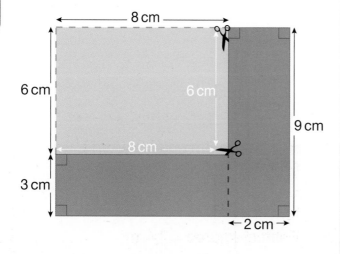

Example

What is the perimeter of the garden lawn?

Think of the lawn as a single rectangle with a 'cut corner'.

$P = 2(L + W)$

$= 2(11 + 10) = 2 \times 21 = 42\,m.$

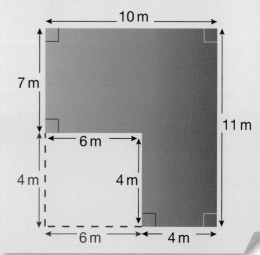

Lesson 3: **Area (1)**

- Calculate the area of rectangles and estimate the area of an irregular shape

Discover

To find the area of a regular shape, count all the squares, or use the formula:
area = length × width.

length

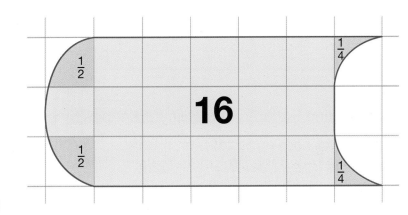

width

Learn

To estimate the area of the irregular shape, we can add the full squares. If less than half a square is covered, do not count it. If more than half a square is covered, count it as 1.

$\frac{1}{2}$ $\frac{1}{4}$

16

$\frac{1}{2}$ $\frac{1}{4}$

Full squares (yellow) = 16

More than half covered (blue) = 2

Total estimated area = 18 cm²

Measure

Example

Estimate the area.

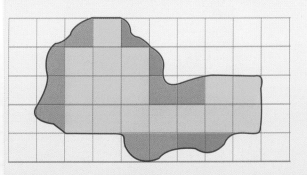

Count full squares (yellow) = 16

Add the squares greater than half (blue) = 8

Do not count the squares less than half (green) = 0.

Estimated area = 24 cm²

Lesson 4: **Area (2)**

- Calculate the area of irregular shapes that are formed by two or more rectangles

Discover

It is sometimes necessary to calculate the area of a compound shape.

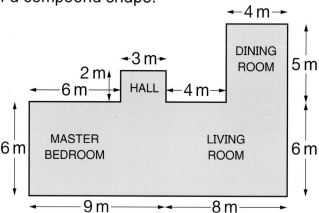

Learn

You can find the area of rectilinear shapes by splitting them into non-overlapping rectangles and finding the sum of their areas.

Or, you can find the area of a 'missing piece' rectangle and subtract this from the larger rectangle.

Example

What is the area of the shape?

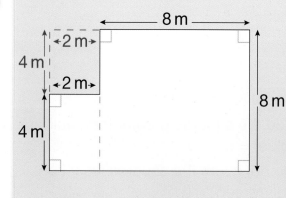

Split the shape into two smaller shapes (green dotted line):

Area = (4 × 2) + (8 × 8)

= 8 + 64

= 72 m²

Alternatively, calculate the area of the larger rectangle (8 m by 10 m) and subtract the 'missing piece' (4 m by 2 m)

Area = (8 × 10) − (4 × 2)

= 80 − 8

= 72 m²

Measure

Lesson 1: **Discrete data**

• Interpret and present discrete data
using bar and pie charts

Key words
• frequency chart
• bar chart
• pie chart

Discover

Learn

Bar charts are used to display discrete data –
data that can only take specific values.

Bar charts have gaps between the bars.

Example

How many more tornadoes took place in 2009/2010
than in 2012/2013?

From the graph:
Number of tornadoes 2009/2010 = 12 + 15 = 27
Number of tornadoes 2012/2013 = 16 + 6 = 22

There were 5 more tornadoes in 2009/2010 than in 2012/2013

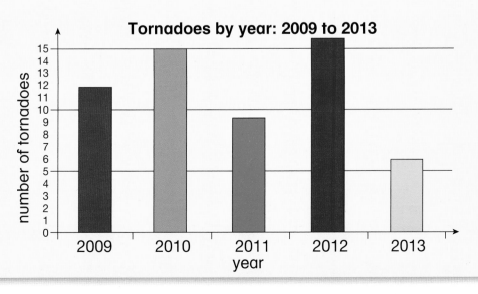

Tornadoes by year: 2009 to 2013

Handling data

Lesson 2: **Continuous data**

• Interpret and present continuous data
  in simple line graphs

Discover

Learn

Line graphs are used for measurements made at regular
time intervals. The quantity measured is recorded on the
vertical axis and time along the horizontal axis.

Example

The graph shows a
company's profits from
2010 and 2015. When did
profits fall?

A fall in profits is shown by
a downward slope of the
line graph.

This occurs between 2011
and 2012, and between
2014 and 2015.

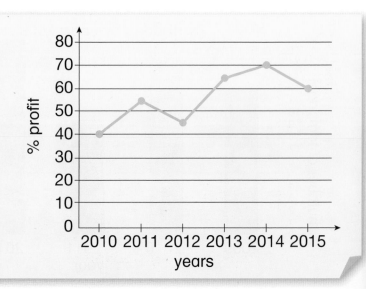

114

Lesson 3: **Solving a problem (1)**

• Solve a problem by interpreting and presenting discrete data using bar and pie charts

Discover

Bar charts and pie charts can be used to represent and interpret the results of a survey.

Learn

When constructing a bar chart, choose a scale where the plotted points use as much of the vertical space as possible. In a pie chart, each section, or 'slice', represents a fraction of the total data.

Example

The manager of a shop wants to know how many of the 100 customers surveyed voted neutral or unsatisfied.

30 (neutral) + 10 (somewhat unsatisfied) + 5 (very unsatisfied) = 45

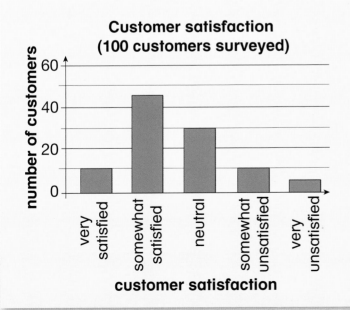

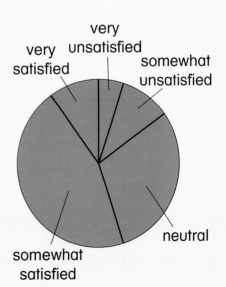

Handling data

Lesson 4: **Solving a problem (2)**

• Solve a problem by interpreting and presenting continuous data in simple line graphs

Discover

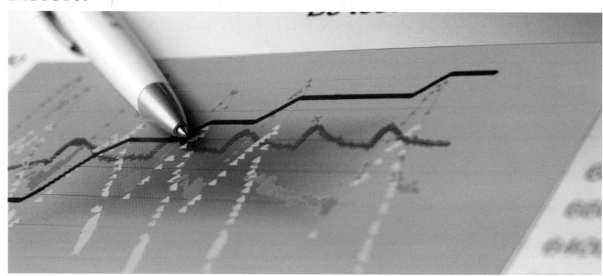

Learn

When creating a line graph, first plot all the points, then join them from one point to the next. Don't try to draw a straight line to connect all the points.

Handling data

Example

The graph shows the growth of a flower from a seed (day 1) to day 10.

Between which two days did the flower show the greatest growth?

The question can be answered in two ways:

i) Compare height measurements for each pair of days to find the biggest difference.

ii) Identify the part of the graph with the steepest slope.

The greatest growth occurred between days 6 and 7.

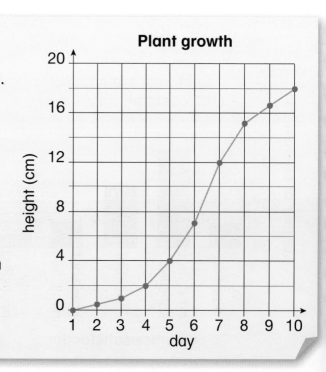

Lesson 5: **Mode and range**

• Find the mode and range of a set of data

Discover

A clothes shop manager needs to know the mode (most popular) size of a T-shirt to ensure there is enough stock.

Learn

To find the mode of a set, count the frequency of each item and identify the value that appears most.

If several values are equally common there will be more than one mode.

The range of a set is the difference between the highest and the lowest values.

Example

Find the mode and range of this set of marks: 2, 4, 7, 9, 2, 7, 4, 3, 7, 2.

Organise the data in a frequency table.

Marks	2	3	4	7	9
Frequency	3	1	2	3	1

2 and 7 have the highest frequency. So, the modes are 2 and 7.

The highest value is 9 and the lowest value is 2.

So, the range is 7 (9 − 2).

Handling data

Lesson 6: **Median and mean**

• Find the median and mean of a set of data

Discover

In this picture the mean number of shopping bags in a group is 2·5 (20 bags divided by 8 groups).

The median is 3.

Learn

The mean, or average, of a set of data is the sum of the data, divided by the number of data.

The median of a data set is found by arranging the numbers in ascending order and picking the middle number.

> For even numbers of data, the median is the mean of the middle two numbers.

Example

Find the mean and median of the following numbers: 3, 3, 5, 5, 6, 6, 7.

$$\text{Mean} = \frac{\text{sum of data}}{\text{number of data values}} = \frac{3 + 3 + 5 + 5 + 6 + 6 + 7}{7} = \frac{35}{7} = 5$$

The median is the middle number: 5

Handling data

Lesson 7: **Probability**

- Use the language of probability to discuss the likelihood of events

> **Key words**
> - certain
> - likely
> - even chance
> - unlikely
> - impossible

Discover

The probability of a flipped coin landing heads is one in two or 50%.

Learn

The probability of an event taking place is somewhere between impossible and certain.

Impossible events have a probability of 0 and certain events have a probability of 1.

Probability is $\frac{1}{2}$ for an even chance event, such as getting heads when flipping a coin.

Handling data

Example

A 1–6 spinner is spun. How likely is it that an odd number will be spun?

The possible outcomes are: 1, 2, 3, 4, 5, 6

Three outcomes are odd: 1, 3, 5

The likelihood of spinning an odd number is three chances out of six, $\frac{3}{6}$ or $\frac{1}{2}$.

The probability is an even chance.

Lesson 8: **Using statistics**

Key words
• statistics
• probability
• pie chart

• Explore how statistics are used in everyday life

Discover

Weather forecasts use data built up over many years.

WEATHER FORECAST

SUN	MON	TUE	WED	THU	FRI	SAT
80°	82°	80°	81°	79°	80°	82°
75°	72°	76°	75°	79°	70°	72°

Learn

Weather forecasts are particularly important in areas where the weather can have a significant, sometimes damaging, effect on life.

Example

How much more likely is it that there will be rain on Thursday compared with Sunday?

Thursday has a 60% chance of rain.

Sunday has a 30% chance of rain.

As 60% is double 30%, the chance of rain is twice as likely.

Tue	Wed	Thu	Fri	Sat	Sun
40%	40%	60%	40%	40%	30%

Handling data

Notes

Notes

Notes

Photo acknowledgements

Every effort has been made to trace copyright holders.

Any omission will be rectified at the first opportunity.

Front cover and title page Katseyephoto/Dreamstime. com, p1 Rawpixel.com/Shutterstock, p4 extender_01/ Shutterstock, p7 Africa Studio/Shutterstock, p10 Designs/Shutterstock, p11 Lessmann/Shutterstock, p12 Ensuper/Shutterstock, p13 Mocha.VP/ Shutterstock, p15 Kostikova Natalia/Shutterstock, p16 ajlatan/Shutterstock, p18 VictorH11/Shutterstock, p20 saiful nizam/Shutterstock, p28 Nerthuz/ Shutterstock, p35 KoQ Creative/Shutterstock, p36 gualtiero boffi/Shutterstock (elephant), p36 Kuttelvaserova Stuchelova/Shutterstock (rat), p36 Jim Hughes/Shutterstock (blue bead), p35 Jiggo_thekop/ Shutterstock (brown beads), p37 mimagephotography/ Shutterstock, p44 Budimir Jevtic/Shutterstock (numbers), p44 Earto/Shutterstock (TV), p44 Davidson Lentz/Shutterstock (saucepan), p44 ffolas/ Shutterstock (chair), p47 m.ekzarkho/Shutterstock (TV), p47 Valentina Proskurina/Shutterstock (teddy bear), p47 Ivonne Wierink/Shutterstock (train), p49 Aksenova Natalya/Shutterstock, p50 The Turtle Factory/Shutterstock, p52 design56/Shutterstock, p56 mariocigic/Shutterstock, p62 HSNphotography/ Shutterstock, p66 Rawpixel.com/Shutterstock, p67 IhorL/Shutterstock, p70 Phovoir/Shutterstock, p72 IVY PHOTOS/Shutterstock, p73 handy/Shutterstock, p75 Dmitri Mikitenko/Shutterstock, p76 Yuliia Liesova/Shutterstock, p77 issarapong srirungpanich/ Shutterstock, p78 Photology1971/Shutterstock, p81 Yurchyks/Shutterstock, p82 Evan Lorne/Shutterstock, p83 Oleg Krugliak/Shutterstock, p84 eskay/ Shutterstock, p87 ergey Dzyuba/Shutterstock, p89 MSSA/Shutterstock, p93 vvoe/Shutterstock (meter ruler), p93 PRILL/Shutterstock (measuring wheel), p93 stimages/Shutterstock (kangaroo road sign), p93 ScofieldZa/Shutterstock (wooden ruler), p93 mexrix/ Shutterstock (no parking road sign), p94 Peter Bernik/ Shutterstock, p95 Olena Yakobchuk/Shutterstock, p98 indigolotos/Shutterstock, p100 David Kay/ Shutterstock, p101 Africa Studio/Shutterstock, p102 Nadalina/Shutterstock, p103 Kitch Bain/ Shutterstock, p104 urbanbuzz/Shutterstock, p107 keport/Shutterstock (clock face), p107 FotoYakov/ Shutterstock (calendar), p108 Jktu_21/Shutterstock, p110 Dim Dimich/Shutterstock, p113 Pressmaster/ Shutterstock, p114 violetkaipa/Shutterstock, p115 sergiophoto/Shutterstock, p116 jean schweitzer/ Shutterstock, p117 ball5/Shutterstock, p118 ?, p119 Alex Kalmbach/Shutterstock, p120 Rommel Canlas/ Shutterstock